This book is for Kaalii

Table of Contents

Preface to the First Edition

This book is the result of a fascination dating back to the age of fifteen or thereabouts, when I first discovered the pleasures of Dashiell Hammett and Raymond Chandler. That was in the era of the Humphrey Bogart revival and of the flowering of interest in American popular art forms, prompted by such things as Pop Art, French auteurist film criticism, and the general air of manic frivolity that surfaced in the mid-sixties. It was a time when publications like *The New York Times Magazine* carried long, uncomfortably serious analyses of phenomena like Camp and Beatlemania.

As a highly serious fifteen-year-old, I did not need to be told that Hammett and Chandler were the real thing—high art free from any taint of what poet Jack Spicer called "the English Department of the spirit." Nowadays, when books like *The Dain Curse* and *The High Window*—not to mention rare *Black Mask* stories by Hammett and fragmented notebook entries by Chandler—are widely available, it is difficult to remember that only a few years ago such titles dropped out of print with predictable regularity. Naturally, the lack of availability made them all the more tantalizing.

To find them involved a search among the racks of old paperbacks outside the secondhand bookshops that lined New York City's Fourth Avenue in those days. Flipping through those hundreds of books slightly less yellowed then than they are today provided a rapid course of instruction in the surefire imagery of several decades of mass marketing; and when the sought-for novels were, at length, reprinted, there was a certain disappointment in realizing that the new editions could not match in intensity those cover paintings of the Forties and Fifties.

As I continued to explore the dimensions of hardboiled fiction in the works of writers like David Goodis and Horace McCoy and James M. Cain, I found that, as often as not, I was buying the books for their artwork as much as for their literary content.

Those early covers were, it seemed, an amazing chronicle of how at least a part of the world was perceived in a postwar era that to my generation had already begun to seem remote. Trivial they might be, but unlike comic books and trading cards they were adult trivia, promising some kind of nitty gritty in place of the glossy vistas offered by the more respectable echelons of mass culture. The paperbacks had flourished through an utter disregard for good taste and moral uplift.

Later, of course, the same publishers would refurbish their tarnished image, and their editions of *Hamlet* and *Silas Marner* would end up as part of the curriculum, in place of the Mickey Spillane or Evan Hunter titles that had once been hidden under many a desktop. The lurid art of the past was replaced by a more lightweight, stylish approach. Suddenly paperback covers were winning graphics awards and their creators were earning recognition as proper members of the world of illustration. But in the process something was lost: the emotional impact of the thousands of explosive canvases commissioned in the heyday of exploitation. In the course of their upward mobility, the paperback publishers had left their roots behind.

The present volume reexamines those tawdry and now almost forgotten books—how they were sold, what they contained, who wrote them, who illustrated them, and what kinds of messages they delivered to the American public. To find the root of those messages, it becomes necessary to explore the American tradition of tough realism, and to ask how real it really was. The novelists—whether their work predated the paperbacks, like Dashiell Hammett and James M. Cain, or whether, like Jim Thompson and John D. MacDonald, they created their books specifically for the paperback format—were the ultimate creators of the visions that were delineated so industriously by the paperback artists.

The paperbacks were a microcosm of American fantasies about the real world. They took the ordinary streets, the dives, the tenements, the cheap hotels, and invested them with mystery—with poetry even—turning them into the stuff of mythology. Shamelessly exploitative, they made their points with a maximum of directness. No trace of subtlety was permitted to cloud the violent and erotic visions that were their essence, and that very lack of subtlety lifted them out of this world. The people they depicted seemed to exist in some impossibly energetic super-America parallel to the one we know.

The covers were voyeuristic rather than decorative. They permitted, by means of a hyperrealism weightier than any photograph could be (after all, a photo would show the people to be mere humans), a peep through a window, and thereby proposed an answer to a society's secret question: What is really going on out there? The answer could not, of course, be pleasing to all. A Congressional committee feared that "the casual reader of such 'literature' might easily conclude that all married persons are habitually adulterous and all teen-agers devoid of any sex inhibitions." Readers today, inured to adultery and uninhibited sex, may still feel considerable qualms about an art that never hesitated to equate sex and violence. The persistent necrophilia is indeed troubling, since the paperbacks were presumably a faithful mirror of the inclinations of the American males for whom they were created. As a man in his forties remarked when looking over some vintage covers, "I got all my sex education from books like this."

In short, they still retain that aura of the forbidden that attaches to anything that spells out the impulses within a society. The inimitable crassness of the covers endures, even in a time when every newsstand carries material more explicit than the Fifties could have anticipated. Over the years the crassness has acquired a comical edge, the inevitable response to an extraordinary mindlessness so blunt and self-assured as to overwhelm. There is something eternal about such one-dimensional images; the attempt to eliminate any possibility of ambiguity leads to an effect of stunning massiveness, even within the tiny dimensions of a paperback cover.

They are, then, little monuments, frozen moments in the history of a culture. Their special appeal is the way they use the materials of everyday life, the surfaces of city streets, rural meadows, small-town public squares, things chosen from what is there, rather than the exoticism of imagined Oriental caravans or Medieval tourneys or interplanetary rockets. They remain fantasies, just as much as those others, but they are fantasies constructed directly from the materials of observed reality. In the same way, the whole tradition of hardboiled fiction, for which the paperbacks proved such a perfect vehicle, built its universe out of pieces of actual speech, actual geography. Here—in these pictures, and in the words they illustrate—is the dream America made of itself, a few decades ago.

Preface to the Second Edition

For this revised and expanded edition, I have taken the opportunity to incorporate additional material, some of which appeared in different form in *The Village Voice*, *The Armchair Detective*, *Paperback Quarterly*, *Paperback Forum*, *Polar*, *I Colori del Nero*, the Lizard Book editions of Jim Thompson and David Goodis, and the French edition of *Hardboiled America*. At the same time I have wherever possible corrected errors and updated passages on the basis of newly available information. The bibliography has been expanded to include some of the most significant writing on areas covered in the book, although in view of the upsurge of recent contributions this can only be a partial listing. The artwork from the first edition (photographed by Dana Levy) has been augmented by some additional covers photographed by Gabriel Burgos.

In looking again at a book written over fifteen years ago, the temptation to intervene, stylistically or intellectually, is strong, and I have sometimes succumbed to it. For the most part, however, I have not attempted to radically revise the tone or the premises of *Hardboiled America* as originally published. Instead, I have added an epilogue in order to consider some of the book's themes in the light of 1996.

I would like to reiterate my gratitude to those who helped with the first edition: James Avati, Thomas L. Bonn, James Eng, Hisako Fujishima, Michael Hooks, Robert Jonas, Everett Raymond Kinstler, Kate Klimo, Paul Kresse, Wendy Lochner, Gerald McConnell, Marion Meese, Stanley Meltzoff, Joel O'Brien, Hans Oldewarris, Dale Phillips, Tom Robbins, Ed Rofheart, Norman Saunders, Harry Schaare, Piet Schreuders, Eliot Weinberger, and Stanley Zuckerberg. Since that time, I have been assisted and enlightened by more people than I could possibly acknowledge here, but I owe a special debt to Michael Barson, Stéphane Bourgoin, Eric Garber, Philippe Garnier, Barry Gifford, François Guérif, Bill O'Connell, Robert Polito, Luc Sante, and Jonathan White.

Chapter One

Icons on Yellowed Paper

Melancholy men lean over dark drinks in yet darker barrooms. Intense redheads roam through empty rooms in glittering negligees. A beefy man raises a clenched fist against a backdrop of drab tenement curtains. Heavy-lidded teenagers crowd a narrow alley. These images, originally designed to pulsate with life, have aged enough so that we are no longer likely to mistake them for part of the real world. The men and women frozen in such portentous tableaux of fear and anguish and violence and desire are now more likely to evoke hearty laughter than the heavy breathing they solicited so strenuously when, newly created, they bared their passion on thousands of newsstands across America.

It is easy enough to see them as farcical relics of an earlier generation's suppressed desires, monsters safely declawed and defanged. But those passionate stances and the artfully rendered settings in which they are framed—alley, tenement, motel room, barroom—were linked, at their origin, to the real feeling of a particular place and time. However heightened, exaggerated, or distorted, the images came from life. They embody a large part of the mythology of their time, a time recent enough to be called our own. Their mood, like that of all myths, is a blend of terror and fascination; and like other myths, it is their fate to be perceived as lurid and absurd by the skeptics who come after. Yet, if we look hard, we can still discern in these toylike figures the heroes and demons of a generation, the enduring archetypes of an era haunted by all-too-real violence and tormented by desire it could not quite fulfill.

Paperbacks such as these, which made their first appearance in 1939 and had their heyday of licentiousness in the decade following the Second World War, were from one point of view merely a physical format, a new way of packaging discount books. But in the unconscious fashion of forms set adrift in a society, they became both a source of new imagery and a synthesis of certain old images that found in them their perfect incarnation. They were a new kind of book, most definitely an American kind of book. The earliest Pocket Books gave rise to paeans of praise to the democratic spirit, praise that would ultimately evolve (sometime in the early Fifties) into cries of horror at the degradation of mass taste.

Although the first paperback publishers strove with reasonable earnestness to provide their public with the finest in world literature, it was inevitably popular taste that triumphed. Popular taste, circa 1939, meant to a large degree whodunits, and the early paperbacks relied heavily on the works of Agatha Christie, Ngaio Marsh, Rex Stout, and other classicists of the mystery genre. But in time it was another brand of crime story—the hardboiled kind, initiated primarily by Dashiell Hammett and carried on industriously by a long line of descendants—that was to become peculiarly identified with the format, so much so that Hammett, even though his last novel was written years before the paperbacks came into existence, can easily be thought of as a "paperback writer."

The hardboiled writers and the paperbacks seemed made for each other. For one thing, embedded in the novels (and no matter how deeply embedded it might be, the publishers would find a way to pry it out) was a vein of tough and sordid realism that lent itself admirably to both illustration and mass exploitation. Furthermore, the quality the novelists aimed for in their writing was manifested in the very form of a paperback book, a book that is compact and casual, a book that can be read and tossed away, that can be carried anywhere—hence, a book on the move, sharing somehow the movement of car or train.

The paperback is light enough to be an extension of yourself, just as the protagonist of the book is your double from the moment you become absorbed in the prose for which you've been readied by the cover's colors and the incantatory jacket copy. In a curious way, the paperback's lightness enables us to bear the heaviness of what occurs inside it. The book has a feathery quality that lets us make light of massacres that might otherwise appall. The paperback—insignificant by definition—serves as a talisman that guides us unharmed through the real world of violence and death.

Artifacts don't choose to become such. It is in the utilitarian fulfillment of their function—in this instance the entertaining of a large public in a period of extreme turbulence and anxiety—that a society's routine throwaways become a reflection of that society, and a teacher to those who approach it from outside. These, certainly, were more immediately imposing than any textbook. In my own case I can remember the fascination exerted, in childhood, by the bold colors and dramatic configurations of who knows what ragged and disreputable paperbacks. They were keys to a mysterious adult world, offering images of lust that, because uncomprehended, showed themselves in a clearer light. Lacking the ability to read the image as intended, the child sees instead a face, a gesture of attack or retreat, a smile forced or buoyant, a stance fraught with energy violent or yielding. The emotions came through with the utmost directness, even if the function was obscure.

The people on the paperback covers lived in a single image, frozen forever in a moment of violence or in a sullen calm preceding the outburst of some unimaginable passion, and had all the more power over a childish imagination because of the singularity of their drama. What came before? What would come after? All was mystery except for the one instant displayed. Against a murky background of menace or erotic suggestion, the human creatures stood out with stunning clarity, sculpted, motionless. Before the grand heroines of tragedy or opera—before Medea and Phèdre and Lucia di Lammermoor—there was the Cora sighted on a dilapidated copy of *The Postman Always Rings Twice*. Each of the covers contained, in fact, a whole drama in itself, sometimes far more evocative than the text it purported to illustrate. Each breathed a strange poetry, which transmuted ever-so-realistic renderings of people and places into ghostly glimpses of a different, and decidedly peculiar, world.

Such art—the art that is flung down at random, pasted on walls, sold for a dime a dozen and forgotten—has a way of permeating its surroundings, and of affecting even those barely conscious that they perceive it. Unlike the art that some critics may yearn for—a self-sufficient structure with clearly defined limits—these everyday creations are inseparable from life, are part of the definition of the particular moment they inhabit. The South Seas paradise with its electric waves and palm trees is inextricably bound up with the pinball machine it decorates, which is an element of the barroom, the barroom in turn being a piece of the larger whole, the city. There is never anywhere to draw the line. In like manner the paperback novel is an object, part of the street on which it's sold, part of the furniture of the house; the colors of its cover as they catch the light as much a part of the landscape as the flowerbed or the skyline beyond.

A child's eyes are more reliable than a critic's mind in such matters, because they cannot help seeing. And if the child does not always perceive what he is meant to perceive, it is because he takes in all the attendant circumstances that, however extraneous, he cannot shut out: so that the Mozart concerto, say, is merely one aspect of a reality that includes the stuffiness of jacket and tie, the polite boredom of adults, the general oppressiveness of the concert hall. On the other hand, the lurid paperback, well-thumbed but hidden on a high shelf, blazes from that shelf like a fire someone has forgotten to extinguish. It lives, and cannot be ignored. From the furtive position of the book on the shelf, the child grasps intuitively the guilt and fascination that surround it.

The effect of such objects when they fall, as the saying goes, into the wrong hands, is as interesting as their effect on the audience for which they were originally intended. From such scraps as these, a child forms notions of history and society, and may ultimately come to feel that a whole philosophy sprang from just such an insignificant seed, a chance image that was never forgotten: a hero whose face was a mask of physical tension that seemed to exclude any possibility of pleasure, or a woman of overwhelming beauty who clutched a revolver in an inexplicably pitiless manner. The images, if they were not real to begin with, become real in the minds of a whole generation of eavesdropping children. These are the images that the world, all unknowing, offers them of itself. They may well become the most loved images, those that announced most clearly and upsettingly the disturbances of the world the children were entering.

Such a culture has always existed, whether in China (in the form of despised tales of ghosts and concubines) or in Medieval Europe (as rough secular farces of lechery and wife beating). The more immediate lineage would include the gothic horror novels of Regency England, the penny dreadfuls of the Victorian period, the dime novels of turn-of-the-century America, the pulps of the Depression. Each gave way to a fresh vision of the lurid underside of life, a vision ever popular and ever in opposition to an official optimism wherein all is sweetness and light.

In nineteenth-century England, poised against pious sentiments and images of cherubic innocence, there were always novels such as *Varney the Vampire, or the Feast of Blood* and penny ballads such as "The Execution of F. G. Manning and Maria, His Wife" (two and a half million copies of which were sold in 1849). An 1853 essay called "On the Literature of the Working Classes" described them in this way: "These are artfully and cleverly dressed up and aided by the depraved pencil of an artist skilled in depicting the sensual and the horrible; and while they interest the tale devourer, they, at the same time, fearfully stimulate the animal propensities of the young, the ardent and the sensual." Such objections would be raised again when, in postwar America, the audience not satisfied by *The Robe* and *My Friend Flicka* turned to *My Gun Is Quick* and *Women's Barracks*. (And in Ireland, where pornography has traditionally been unknown, it was common not long ago to find the vast run of books bearing the imprimatur of the Church sold alongside imported copies of *True Detective*, with their tales of decapitated corpses.)

This subversive longing for all that is not nice raises all sorts of moral questions which I will try to refrain from either asking or answering. A host of concerned parents and earnest utopians has perennially proposed, as a neat solution to an enormous array of social ills, the suppression of images that feed the popular appetite for violence and undiscriminating lust. An extreme example of this approach is Dr. Frederic Wertham's *Seduction of the Innocent* (1954), an intense and unfailingly humorless diatribe against comic books which effectively brought about the suppression of the EC line of horror comics in the mid-Fifties. Wertham is a particularly absurd instance, but in his zeal for the regulation of popular culture he has plenty of company at all points along the political spectrum. Such proponents have over the years questioned whether such things as the Executioner novels of Don Pendleton or *The Texas Chainsaw Massacre* had a role to play in the ideal commonwealth. Curiously enough, many absolute rulers have shared this distaste for violent melodrama, feeling perhaps that it detracted from the real-life melodramas they were in the process of enacting. Cromwell did away with the English theatre. The Nazis sanctioned Viennese operettas but condemned gangster movies. Films made under Stalin's rule were overwhelmingly sentimental and free of overt violence. In Mao's China, dramatic expression was restricted to stylized ballet movements, and detective stories—even those with ideologically sound heroes—were criticized for lauding the prowess of an individual at the expense of collective endeavor.

On the other hand, this doesn't mean one should necessarily applaud the extraordinary delight in torture and bloodletting that is given free rein in the laissez-faire cinemas of America, Japan, or Hong Kong. The problem of where to establish limits remains unresolved, and is made thornier by the ease with which the mind condones sanctified violence—be it in *Henry V*, *Alexander Nevsky*, *The Green Berets*, or *Taking Tiger Mountain by Strategy*. The fundamentally indistinguishable specifics of bone breakage and blood flow are redeemed time and again by having the proper label affixed to them.

It can at least be said that this is tricky terrain where it is difficult to tell friend from foe. The German crime melodramas of the anti-Fascist Fritz Lang were scripted by his wife, the card-carrying National Socialist Thea von Harbou. Dashiell Hammett used the mechanics of the private-eye novel to make a critique of capitalist America; Mickey Spillane employed the same mechanics pioneered by Hammett in the service of a ferocious sadism. With historical irony, Sam Spade's literary descendant Mike Hammer was kicking in the teeth of Commie subversives while Sam Spade's creator was going to prison for refusing to testify against Leftist associates. And when Robert Aldrich, in filming *Kiss Me, Deadly* (1955), perpetrated an ironic reversal of Spillane's brutal fantasy in which hero was metamorphosed into villain, there were few who got the point—and of those few, some wondered if it really made any difference.

Certainly it made no difference to the paperback publishers, who sold a Hammett or a Spillane in the same untroubled, bludgeoning fashion, prompting a Marxist illustrator of the period, who considers Hammett "an American genius," to call his paperback publishers "the original smut peddlers." (The artists I spoke with while preparing this book were often eager to expose the unscrupulousness of their former employers.) It was their marketing savvy that reduced *The Sun Also Rises* to a single blurb—"Could he live without the power to love?"—and summarized Faulkner's *The Wild Palms* in the image of a swimsuited maiden posed against a beach parasol.

But the case is not quite the simple one of Ruthless Exploiters vs. Sensitive Artists. After all, Dashiell Hammett himself wrote the syndicated comic strip *Secret Agent X-9* and (in part) the radio series *The Adventures of Sam Spade*, while William Faulkner worked on the scripts of *The Road to Glory* and *Land of the Pharaohs*—and no one has suggested that either was on the brink of starvation at the time. While some critics may once have found it easy to make a clean distinction between the accomplished art of *Red Harvest* and *Sanctuary* (both of which were considered something less than cultural monuments when first published) and such supposedly expendable trash as *Secret Agent X-9* or *Land of the Pharaohs*, in the American cultural web they are interwoven densely and inextricably.

The paperbacks provide just such a stew of high and low, vigorous and decayed; they are the common ground of Shakespeare and Irving Shulman and Bishop Fulton J. Sheen, of *Light in August* and *Lust Party*, indiscriminately mingled and mated. In short, they partake of the characteristic American atmosphere. It is useless to distinguish among "high art," "personal art," "folk art," "commercial art," or "exploitation"; in the living situation, they all float about in the same pond.

Doubtless exploitation was largely the intent of the boys in charge of operations (although closet idealists were not unknown). The corporate approach to cover art was summed up by George Axelrod in his 1952 play *The Seven Year Itch*. The hero, the marketing director of a paperback house, is describing a forthcoming edition of *The Scarlet Letter*: "Mr. Brady wants to change *The Scarlet Letter* to *I Was an Adulteress*. I know it all seems a little odd to you—but Mr. Brady understands the twenty-five-cent book field. . . . The cover will be a picture of Hester Prynne with a cigarette hanging out of her mouth. She'll be in a real tight, low-cut dress. Our big problem is—if the dress is cut low enough to sell any copies, there won't be any space on the front for a big red letter. . . ."

From one point of view, the paperbacks can be seen as just another aspect of the media bombardment to which Americans have (with no apparent unwillingness) been increasingly subjected. What other culture has had its fantasies depicted for it in such profusion and in such a variety of forms? The most determined cultural archaeologist cannot cope with the flood of material that the marketing directors of America have come up with: pulps, comic books, paperbacks, movies, television shows, record albums, trading cards, radio programs, stamp books, coloring books, posters, illustrated lunch-boxes, illustrated T-shirts, decals, badges, laser beam concerts. The list goes on and becomes ever more inventive as technology discovers new ways of delighting the senses of the citizenry.

No doubt, nearly all of it is being carefully stored away for purposes of future analysis. Older cultures looked on the matter somewhat differently. In his *Early Chinese Literature*, Burton Watson writes of the ancient Chinese: "Vulgar, stupid, or rustic, on the other hand, were their terms for any kind of writing that seemed to them absurd or shallow in content or uncouth in expression . . . The vulgar type of writings they ignored or preserved only for curiosity's sake. Thus most of this literature has been lost, or even deliberately destroyed . . . We have, for example, no collections of popular folk tales or works on sexual regimen."

The modern scholar is aghast at such destruction of valuable source materials, but no doubt the Chinese felt they were doing future generations a favor by sparing them a heap of ephemera. In effect, they were cleaning the place up and taking out the trash before the next tenants moved in. The contemporary American researcher, on the other hand, is adamant in insisting that not one Shirley Temple vehicle, not one Buster Brown comic, shall be lost to posterity. As the onlooker remarks in Charles Addams' cartoon of robots manufacturing robots in the robot factory: "Sometimes I ask myself, 'Where will it ever end?'"

Indeed, the works of Dashiell Hammett and Raymond Chandler have promised to become as rich a lode for academicians as those of Herman Melville or James Joyce. Concurrently, early paperbacks have become yet another field for collectors of the transitory, joining the company of *Plastic Man* comics, cans of James Bond's 007 Malt Liquor, Coca-Cola placemats, and Zorro cards. It is only in relatively recent years that the world has been beating a path to the doors of the musty secondhand bookstores—and yard sales, barn sales, and garage sales—where, if you are lucky, you might still find a copy of an authentically lurid edition of *Double Indemnity* or *The Lady in the Lake*. But don't wait too long. Even if the collectors don't beat you to the punch—and even if the barns and bookstores themselves don't pass entirely into oblivion—in a few years' time such a book may well have crumbled to dust. The collector of hardboiled novels is often faced with the dilemma of whether to read the book and watch it disintegrate into small pieces as each page is turned, or else preserve it unread but intact.

These books were not intended by their publishers to endure, but merely to fill a few hours for someone looking for entertainment a bit grittier than the more official culture of the time, those elaborate glories of the Forties and Fifties that have since been recapitulated almost to exhaustion: the ceremonial music of big bands and crooners, the grand rituals of television history, the formal splendor of never-to-be-forgotten MGM musicals—in brief, the world as reconstituted by *Life* magazine, a world ultimately reassuring and meaningful.

In that light the hardboiled tradition, and the paperbacks that amplified it and distributed it to a growing audience, seems to have played a subversive role. These novels, and the covers that illustrate them, speak of the ignoble corners of life beyond the glow of Jane Powell, *Father Knows Best*, and the healthy, smiling faces in magazines advertising milk or frozen dinners or trips to California. An arsenal of media had been assembled to project the image of a nation prosperous and secure, of citizens steeped in homegrown virtues and showered with material blessings.

The paperbacks, on the other hand, tell of a dark world below the placid surface, a world whose inhabitants tend to be grasping, dissatisfied, emotionally twisted creatures. Here, all is not well; from the looks of it, all could not be much worse. This other America, when it is not a bleak rural wasteland inhabited by murderous primitives, is a glittering hell ruled by money and violence, flaunting images of beauty that are either deceptive or unobtainable. The temple of this world is the barroom, and its holy of holies the booth where the blonde sits, always just out of reach. The precincts are guarded not by priests but by cool psychopathic bodyguards who wisecrack as they bludgeon. It is a world whose governing forces are, as in the title of a film of the era, *Fear and Desire*.

Worse yet, at the heart of it all, there is an implied lack of meaning. Unlike the settling of the West or the Second World War, the events transcribed by hardboiled fiction serve no particular purpose; they just happen. A nation gets the epic it deserves, and not necessarily the one it wants. Certainly the characteristically cool and cynical tone of the tough-guy novels was a distinctly American invention, a music that seems to have created itself out of its surroundings. It represented an antidote to an equally prevalent American penchant for bombast and self-glorification, as evident in the earliest effusions of patriotic oratory as in the latest brand of hype for oil companies or television networks. One of the primary services of the hardboiled novel has been the deflation of such rhetoric. From Hammett to Ross Macdonald, we have been cautioned again and again to beware of the forked tongues of politicians, preachers, lawyers, and movie producers, as we would beware of a vacuum-cleaner salesman. In place of their sickly-sweet reassurance, there is offered no sustaining message, no heroic struggle—just a hard, bitter silence, a determination to *act,* even if the action takes place in a void, a long stare at an unloving landscape.

America once used the word *hucksterism* to describe a phenomenon that was then perceived as something of an alien encroachment. The phenomenon is now so endemic that the phrase *American culture* might as well be substituted for it. The early paperbacks demonstrate in crude form the effects of the nascent advertising/packaging/marketing revolution in one particular area—the retailing of literature (although to today's pros, they are of course embarrassingly primitive). It is ironic that such writers as Hammett and Chandler, profoundly opposed to the hucksterish tendencies of their day, should have found such a natural home in the exploitative paperbacks, a home far more natural than any future academic embalming could be.

If, despite everything, the early paperbacks convey a somehow democratic mood, it is perhaps because their publishers worked under circumstances anarchic enough to permit a few unexpected and remarkable freedoms. The paperback industry of their day was a relatively loose and improvisational affair, compared with today's gigantic and highly sophisticated structure. As if by accident, that ramshackle industry presided over one of those shifts that indicate a culture's course before it has even discovered it for itself. Many people contribute to such shifts: each writer, as he plugs himself into the collective mythology and filters it through his own consciousness; each painter, as he sets out to depict scenes from that mythology, like a more ancient artist sketching according to a preordained format the hieratic emblems of some Gospel or Sutra.

The texts and images thus created are simple if considered in isolation, but ultimately complex in the unforeseen interrelations among them or between a given image and the "real" life it purports to show. The paperback industry, like all the other image machines of America, is dedicated to the creation of an eternal present. In the very act of reflecting reality, it seeks to create a new reality, one in which all eyes are focused on its hall of mirrors. Past and future are of no account; what matters is only the one enormous Now of the spectator immersed in his spectacle.

But an assemblage of the images the machine has emitted at various moments becomes a clear chart that lets us navigate through history, since each image is located in a definite place and at a precise instant. This book is an attempt to isolate one such locus, and to identify the transformations that occurred within it.

Chapter Two

Origins of the Paperbacks

Cheap reprints and books bound in paper arose and flourished sporadically in America from the nineteenth century onwards. Although most of these were purely commercial efforts, a significant percentage were associated with a zeal for bringing culture to the masses. Nevertheless, and despite the obvious practicality of cheap mass printings, no one had been able to give that kind of publishing any permanence until June 19, 1939, when the first ten releases of Pocket Books saw the light of day. Robert DeGraff, the company's founder, may have been influenced by the success of Penguin Books, which had begun publishing in England in 1935.

The kickoff of the paperback industry was heralded by a full-page ad in *The New York Times*: "OUT TODAY—THE NEW POCKET BOOKS THAT MAY REVOLUTIONIZE AMERICA'S READING HABITS." According to publishing historian John Tebbel's account, DeGraff later recalled: "We had a little argument over the ad. I wanted to say WILL REVOLUTIONIZE . . . but everybody seemed to feel that was too strong, so we compromised on 'may.'" Success was virtually instantaneous. For one thing, DeGraff knew his market. The first ten titles were canny choices, a carefully mixed bag of culture, uplift and entertainment: William Shakespeare and Agatha Christie, James Hilton's *Lost Horizon* and Dorothea Brande's *Wake Up and Live!* Most of the ten would be reprinted again and again.

And the format was brilliant. Pocket Books were not merely books bound in paper; they were not merely cheap, like the gloomy blue-bound hardback reprints that sold in those days for a dollar, books that gave you—in small type crammed into double columns—the collected works of Zola or Kipling or Plutarch in a form suitably ungratifying to the eye, a form somber enough to remind you of all the weight attaching to a Classic, thus catering to a reverence for learning from which the idea of pleasure had been for all time excluded.

Pocket Books, on the other hand, were fun: they fit snugly in the hand; the shape immediately differentiated them from other books; and from behind the unmistakable Perma-Gloss coating gleamed the original paperback covers, first of all the silvery blue terraces of Shangri-La. As the slogan had it, they were "kind to your pocket and your pocketbook." They were also durable: paper and binding were of superior quality, so that a 1940 Pocket Book is more likely to be in one piece today than the average 1960 paperback.

For a number of years Pocket Books had the field to itself. "Pocket Book" became a generic term for paperback (a word that had yet to be invented), and the imprint's colophon, Gertrude the Kangaroo, became as much a fixture of American commercial folklore as Elsie the Cow or the Philip Morris bellboy. In fact, as the fortunes of the company expanded, Gertrude went through several incarnations, culminating in today's barely recognizable version—a severely depersonalized, streamlined creature whose profile, caught in mid-jog, seems appropriate to the computerized slickness of today's paperbacks. As John Tebbel ex-

plains it, that original Gertrude—a bespectacled, somewhat stodgy kangaroo with one book in hand and another in pouch—was designed by Frank J. Lieberman, who named her after his mother-in-law. He was paid $25 for his pen-and-ink sketch. In 1943, Walt Disney Studios redesigned the colophon, producing a livelier creature stylistically akin to the other Disney creations. This design was later modified by the removal of the baby kangaroo and the glasses (because they appeared to suggest that the typeface of the books was hard to read). The difference in tone between Lieberman's original design and the Disney remake suggests very well the rapid expansion of the paperback industry; the original has a distinctly homemade quality, whereas Disney's version irons out all the rough spots to produce a far more perfect and self-conscious marketing device.

As progenitor of the paperbacks, Pocket Books enjoyed a certain cachet of respectability denied to the others who joined the field later. Where others focused on mysteries and on anything with a hint of salacity, Pocket Books maintained a list of catholic appeal in keeping with the company's swift evolution into that unmistakable thing, an American Institution. The old Pocket Books lists offer an astonishing assortment of items, *The Rubaiyat of Omar Khayyam* side by side with *Hugger-Mugger in the Louvre*, *Pride and Prejudice* ("Read the story of the movie that featured Laurence Olivier and Greer Garson!") and *The Pocket Book of Dog Stories* ("Only MacKinlay Kantor could write an introduction to make you fully realize the relationship of man and dog").

They were definitely there to minister to all the literary needs of their public, which was designed to include everybody, just as the list seems intended to make all other publishers superfluous. There was no end of testimonials from the great and celebrated—Lowell Thomas, William Lyon Phelps, W. Somerset Maugham, Moss Hart ("the greatest invention since the steamboat"), Paul de Kruif ("the millions you reach are the salt of the earth, that take life seriously"), and Dale Carnegie ("How I wish Pocket Books had been in existence when I was a boy plowing corn on a Missouri farm. I wept then because I couldn't afford to buy $2.00 books").

A new domain of literature had been created, governed with benign exclusiveness by Pocket Books. But this happy monopoly could not endure forever. In 1941 Avon Books came on the scene, and was promptly hauled off to court by Pocket for infringement of their format. Ultimately Avon was ordered to desist from use of the word "pocket" in its blurb and advertising. (On a typical early Avon title, the phrase "Avon *pocket-size* Books"—Avon's italics—occurs six times.) Aside from this purely technical victory, Pocket actually suffered a defeat, having lost its solitary lordship over the paperback industry. Once Avon had established that the paperback format was no one's personal property, others were quick to get in the act: Popular Library (1942), Dell (1943), Bantam (1945), Graphic (1948), Pyramid (1949), Lion (1949), Checker (1949), and New American Library (1949). New American Library was in fact new in name only—it had been operating in America since 1939 as the American branch of Penguin Books, under the guidance of Ian Ballantine, Victor Weybright, and refugee German publisher Kurt Enoch.

Avon did not spare the hype in marketing its new product, going into remarkable detail about its physical properties: "Bound in heavy weight covers, they have a delightful flexibility in handling, and stand up well under reading and rereading. The covers are specially processed to make them resistant to dirt, damp, and rough usage; and can easily be washed clean. And finally, the books are colorfully stained on all three sides with fast book dyes, serving to keep the pages free of dust. AVON BOOKS are grand books in every way—and every AVON volume carries its distinctive hall-mark: the SHAKESPEARE-HEAD." This latter was a haggard face, allegedly Shakespeare's, that for many years peered from the title page and back cover of such titles as *A Homicide for Hannah*, *Loose Ladies*, and Hector France's alluringly titled *Musk, Hashish and Blood*.

But the books, despite the claims to the contrary, were a decidedly inferior product to Pocket Books. Unlike the Pockets, the early Avons tend to disintegrate nowadays (if one actually tries to read them) into a heap of brittle yellowed fragments, just like those priceless collections of pulp magazines that sit in temperature-controlled rooms and can

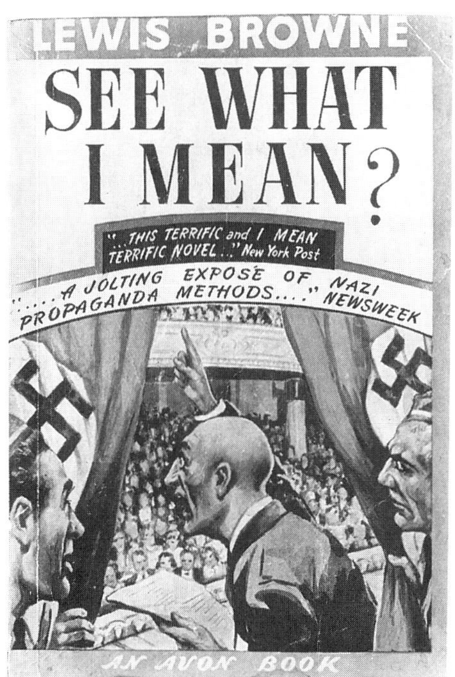

Avon 54 (1944)

Avon 94 (1946)

Avon 38 (1943)

Avon 124 (1947)

never be read by anyone. Avon emulated the pulps in other ways; its covers made the same kind of blatant come-on, and paved the way for the great lurid outpouring of the postwar years.

The artistic quality of these anonymously executed covers was generally poor—the draftsmanship compares unfavorably with any but the cheapest pulps. Every now and again, a detail shows some care. For instance, the transparent black lingerie on *Murder Comes First* (1951) is treated with devoted skill compared with the "face" of the man coming through the doorway. Again, on *Hope of Heaven* (1950) the waves of glowing blonde hair have considerably more vitality than the faces of either of the protagonists—and these are already an improvement on earlier Avon covers. Still, these paintings have a strong appeal, stronger than many "better" covers executed for Pocket Books. Avon's unapologetic vulgarity ultimately proved more powerful than the more sensitive efforts of its competitor.

As for the literature these covers adorned, the list was by no means trashy. Avon's early authors included William Faulkner (*Mosquitoes*), Raymond Chandler (*The Big Sleep*, *Five Murderers*, *Five Sinister Characters*), Noel Coward (*To Step Aside*), James M. Cain (*Double Intdemnity*, *The Embezzler*, *Career in C Major*), Ben Hecht (*Count Bruga*), and John O'Hara (*Doctor's Son*, *Hope of Heaven*, *Butterfield 8*)—an interesting sampling of the fiction of the period, with enough spice to justify those alluring cover paintings. Unlike Pocket Books, Avon kept inspirational and educational titles to a minimum, thus foreshadowing the ultimate triumph of sex in the paperback marketplace.

Meanwhile the war had begun, and while wartime restrictions curtailed the expansion of the industry (as well as lowering the quality of the paper used), the portable nature of paperbacks made them naturals for GI reading matter. This in turn gave the publishers patriotic motives for hyping their books. All literature, even the lowest forms of escapism, had now been glorified in the name of morale. Each publisher had its own way of delivering the message. According to Avon, "Because the New Avon Books are easy to open, light to hold, thrilling to read and compact to carry or store in clothing or bags, they are ideal as gifts to the boys in the Armed Forces." Dell seemed to compensate for the

lightweight nature of its list with a more somber pronouncement: "BOOKS ARE WEAPONS—in a free democracy everyone may read what he likes. Books educate, inform, inspire; they also provide entertainment, bolster morale. This book has been manufactured in conformity with wartime restrictions—read it and pass it on."

Pocket Books urged its readers to "share this book with someone in uniform," while opposite the title page, above the words THIS IS A WARTIME BOOK, a streamlined eagle clutching a thick volume in its talons proclaimed: BOOKS ARE WEAPONS IN THE WAR OF IDEAS. The mobilization of publishing was widely evident, as in the Fighting Forces Penguin Specials produced as a joint venture by Penguin Books and *Infantry Journal.* Even more striking were the Armed Forces Editions, an exceptionally well-edited series of unusually shaped books specially designed to fit snugly into military pockets.

Wartime sales indicate the extent to which people were using books to escape from the war. It was undoubtedly during—if not because of—the war that the paperbacks won full market acceptance. Nevertheless, the industry was tiny by today's standards. In 1945 the number of paperback titles in print totaled 112. By the next year the figure had risen to 353, and by 1951 to 866. Unfortunately, this postwar expansion coincided with a severe drop in sales. Evidently the newly returned GIs had other things to occupy themselves with than perusing every new Pocket Book. Had paperbacks been merely a novelty that had now worn thin? A mild panic seized the now crowded marketplace, and was soon manifested in the new look in covers. The comparatively restrained cover art of Pocket Books and American Penguin no longer sufficed; Art Deco abstractions and cityscapes in the manner of Stuart Davis gave way very quickly to photographic realism and expanses of bared flesh. "As competition increased," wrote Frank Schick, "covers became gaudier, colors brighter, and women's attire on the cover picture more scanty." This abrupt stylistic change was to boost sales in the short run, and in the long run to tarnish the respectability of the hitherto innocuous paperbacks.

On all sides it was the heyday of the lurid. Mickey Spillane was triumphing over all competitors with his brand of unleashed sadism, and Hollywood was making the most of its newly refurbished style of exhibitionism (*The Outlaw*) and violence (*Kiss of Death*). Wars in America have generally led to a relaxation of sexual censorship; for instance, the public acceptability of *Penthouse* and *Hustler* can probably be traced to the Vietnam War. Likewise, the returning GIs of the 1940s craved stronger stuff than Betty Grable pinups. A new roughness was evident. With all the energy of an industry undergoing rapid development, the paperbacks—free of the constraints that hampered movies and radio—resolutely pushed the limits. For all their previous contributions to troop morale and the education of the masses, the paperbacks were no longer "nice." Encouraged by rising sales figures, they were no longer playing by the same rules. (An illustrator whose career began in the postwar period recalls, "The word went out—get sex into it somehow.")

The covers were designed to leap at the eye of someone casually passing a newsstand or soda-fountain book rack. Once the potential buyer had gotten close enough to pick up the book, the copy took over. The gaudy colors and flagrant lasciviousness of the covers aimed only at projecting visibility among the dozens of other similar covers all crying for attention. Indeed, to fully appreciate the aesthetics of an old paperback cover, it should be contemplated from a distance of twenty to thirty feet.

The need for maximum intensity and readability engendered forms of stunning unsubtlety, like Paul Kresse's remarkable painting for *It's a Crime* (Pocket Books, 1951), in which the butt of a revolver—of mammoth proportions and trailing visible streaks of air—whizzes past a man's head, as the victim's face tightens in agony. It has, one might say, impact. The yellow-on-red copy offers the superfluous commentary: "My gun-butt smashed his skull!"

Provocation took a number of standard forms, which publishers showed no reluctance to use again and again. The most frequently encountered image is the woman holding a cigarette (*Whistle Stop*, *Galatea*) or the woman in the bedroom, half-undressed, the man usually a passive observer (*Kiss Tomorrow Goodbye*, *Cassidy's Girl*, *Everybody Does It*). A second, more unsettling category involved violence against women. No hesitation was shown about exploiting the erotic potential of a corpse (*The Case of the Red Box*, *The Four False Weapons*) on reprints of what were in fact extremely staid traditional whodunits. A final and surprisingly frequent motif is that of a woman holding a gun, usually (*A Dame Called Murder*) to threaten a man, although on Rudolph Belarski's memorably absurd cover for *Dark Threat* (Popular Library, 1951) it is directed against another woman.

Nineteen fifty-one marked the high-water mark for such imagery. Year after year, the publishers had vied with each other to extract all the eroticism possible from a limited set of ingredients, and the strain on their imaginations was becoming obvious. At the same time, this orgy of flying fists and diaphanous lingerie could not go on forever without meeting resistance. An apologetic tone began to creep into publishers' statements. Even Popular Library, responsible for some of the most lurid cover art of all, felt obliged to justify itself: "This book, like all Popular Library titles, has been carefully selected by the Popular Library Editorial Board for its literary substance and entertainment value."

Such disclaimers were hardly enough. A new spirit of repression and censorship was being felt in the land; having already feasted on domestic Communism in its various forms, it now sought fresh prey. Groups like the National Organization of Decent Literature eagerly fanned the flames of hysteria. The Detroit vice squad, notorious for its thuggish interpretation of the First Amendment, seized a multitude of paperbacks. The national hunt for "alien-minded radicals and moral perverts" (in the words of a U.S. Senator of the period) had branched out from the specifically political to become a kind of cultural revolution. Everything from soft-core pornography (of the *Shanty Town Tease* variety) to

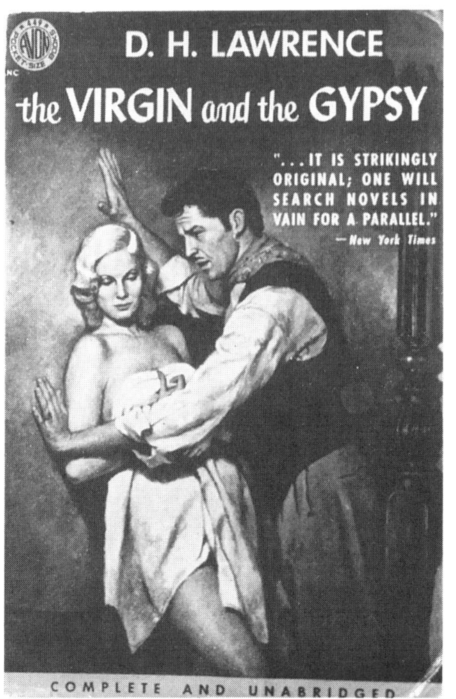

Avon 449 (1952)
Artist: Victor Olson

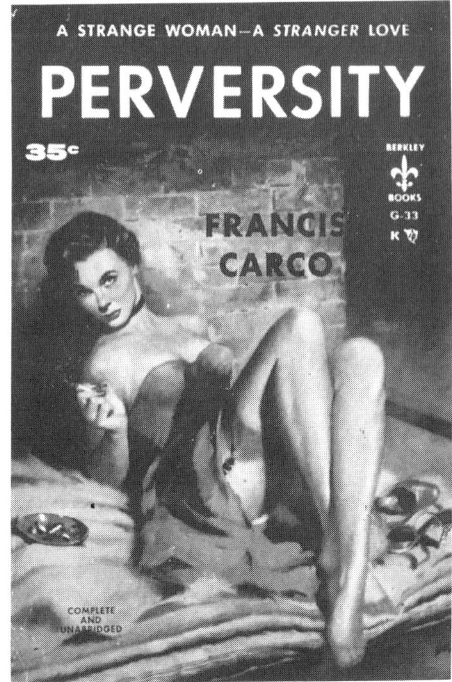

Berkley G-33 (1956)

Bantam 423 (1949)
Artist: Tom Lovell

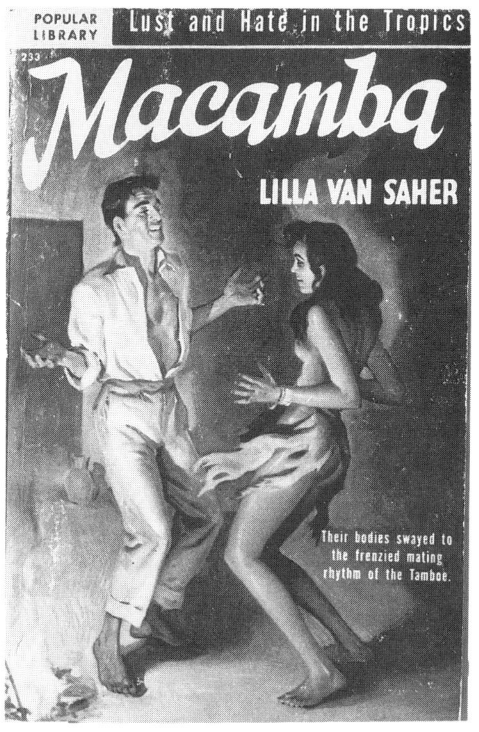

Popular Library 233 (1950)

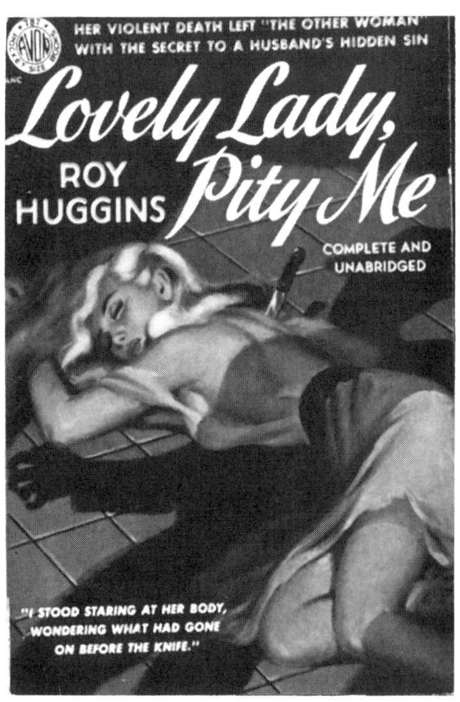

Avon 282 (1951)

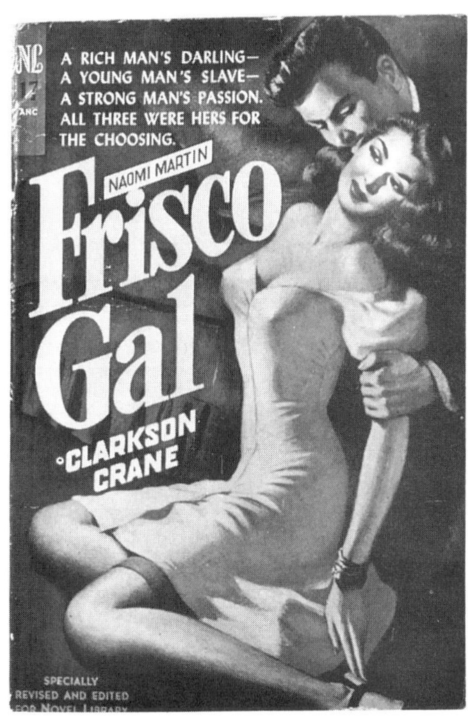

Novel Library 17 (1949)

Avon T-216 (1958)

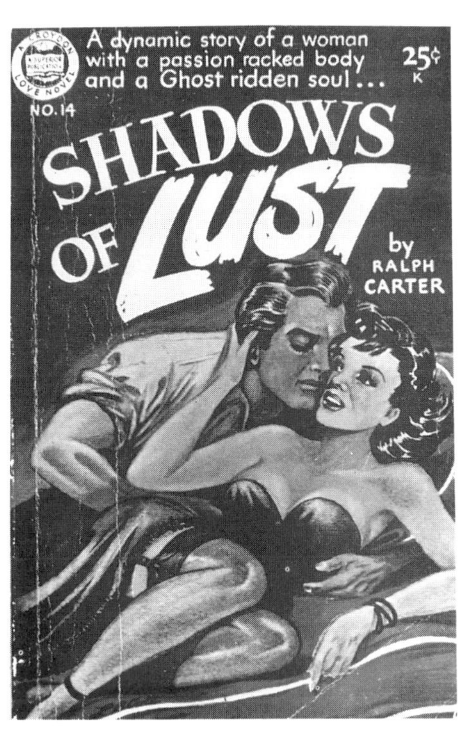

Croydon Love Novel 14 (1951)
Artist: L. B. Cole

mass-market editions of D. H. Lawrence and Aldous Huxley were to be purged from the body of the Republic, presumably to leave nothing in their wake but Gideon Bibles and civil-defense pamphlets.

By 1952 the paperback industry found itself under investigation by the House Select Committee on Current Pornographic Materials. Their report is a document rich in the unwitting comedy so often provided by the would-be Savanarolas of the American heartland. The witnesses, nearly all of them "friendly," included a priest, a vice-squad official, and a heroic newstand dealer. All were generous in the kind of self-righteousness and flag waving associated with such investigations.

Ultimately the paperbacks (as well as the committee's other primary targets, girlie magazines and comic books) were denounced in resounding anathemas:

> Some of the most offensive infractions of the moral code were found to be contained in the low-cost, paper-bound publications known as "pocket-size books." . . . The so-called pocket-size books, which originally started out as cheap reprints of standard works, have largely degenerated into media for the dissemination of artful appeals to sensuality, immorality, filth, perversion, and degeneracy. The exaltation of passion above principle and the identification of lust with love are so prevalent that the casual reader of such "literature" might easily conclude that all married persons are habitually adulterous and all teen-agers completely devoid of any sex inhibitions.

That pretty well captures the tone of the proceedings. On a less strident note, Rep. Katherine St. George of New York indulged in one revealing bit of wistful naivete: "I can remember very well that ten years ago so-called smutty literature was unknown in this country. . . . I was always under the very happy impression that Americans did not read this kind of literature, but they apparently do."

Cover art naturally came in for a large share of the condemnation. The committee urged the eradication of what were coyly dubbed "the 3 S's"—i.e., sex, sadism, and the smoking gun. The report further noted that "some of the publishers of sex stories found that by encompassing their filth, or near filth, behind the most lurid and daring illustrations of voluptuous young women on the covers, book sales increased dramatically. In some cases the outside covers are more salaciously suggestive than the reading matter inside."

The dramatic highpoint of the hearings came when John O'Connor, Chairman of the Board of Bantam Books, was called to the stand. O'Connor, a highly articulate man and head of what was then one of the best-edited and most "respectable" paperback houses, found himself locked in confrontation with the inexorable Representative Edward Rees of Kansas. The testimony is worth quoting at length for the theatricality of its repartee:

> MR. BURTON [H. Ralph Burton, consultant to the committee]. Have you read these books, Mr. O'Connor [referring to certain Bantam Books in evidence]?
>
> MR. O'CONNOR. Let's see. I have read *Don't Touch Me* [a then-controversial novel by MacKinlay Kantor], and perhaps that is a good one for your purpose.
>
> MR. REES. You say that is a good one?
>
> MR. O'CONNOR. I thought it might be a good one.
>
> MR. BURTON. For our purpose.
>
> MR. REES. What do you say about it? Is it good for the public?
>
> MR. O'CONNOR. Am I being questioned now on the contents of the book?
>
> MR. REES. Yes. You said it was good for us, and I am asking you.
>
> MR. O'CONNOR. I sensed from what I read of the earlier hearings, that the committee is searching for books which, in its opinion, tend toward the pornographic side, but that does not by any means mean that I agree with the committee.
>
> MR. REES. What I want to know is, do you approve that book for reading?
>
> MR. O'CONNOR. I can't answer the question, that question, "yes" or "no," because that is a question—
>
> MR. REES. Do you think it is a good book for the public to read?
>
> MR. O'CONNOR. I do; yes.
>
> MR. REES. And you approve that sort of stuff?
>
> MR. O'CONNOR. May I expand my answer?

MR. REES. Well, I just asked you if you said that is good; that is the end of it. It is either good or bad.

MR. O'CONNOR. I believe, if this book is not pornographic, if it is not pornographic—

MR. REES. Do you think the material is good, the reading of it is good?

MR. O'CONNOR. I think MacKinlay Kantor is a very distinguished author.

MR. REES. I am not talking about MacKinlay Kantor; I am talking about the material in that book. Do you think it is good for folks to read?

MR. O'CONNOR. If they wish to read it.

MR. REES. Do you think it is good for children?

MR. O'CONNOR. I think the only question is whether it is pornographic.

MR. REES. That is not the only question. I am just asking you, do you think children ought to read that book?

MR. O'CONNOR. I don't think I would give it to my daughter to read, for example, if that is the answer you want from me.

MR. REES. Well, that is one of the answers; yes.

MR. O'CONNOR. I don't think this particular book is one that it is a good thing for adolescents to read, no; I do not.

MR. REES. Do you think it is good for anybody to read? Do you think it is something that does a fellow good?

MR. O'CONNOR. If a man wishes to read it, why not, or a woman, an adult person.

MR. REES. So you think it is all right to put that out?

MR. O'CONNOR. I think so. Why not?

MR. REES. Well, if you would read the thing you would know why not.

MR. O'CONNOR. Would you let me make a statement of my opinion with respect to this book?

MR. REES. Answer whether it is a good thing to put out on the newsstands for sale to the public.

MR. O'CONNOR. For adults, why not?

MR. REES. Because of the stuff that is in it.

MR. O'CONNOR. Well, that is your opinion, Mr. Rees. . . . This book is published under a constitutional guarantee and it is also subject to prosecution under the pornography statutes if it is a pornographic book. If it is a pornographic book, then it should be suppressed and the publisher should be punished and the distributor should be punished.

THE CHAIRMAN. What do you think, Mr. O'Connor, this committee was formed for? Had there been such a congressional committee prior to this time?

MR. O'CONNOR. Happily not.

THE CHAIRMAN. To ferret out this kind of trash?

MR. REES. Did you say "happily not ?

MR. O'CONNOR. Yes; because I think the testimony before this committee has been entirely one-sided.

One way or another the crusaders got their wish. There was no overt censorship, but intense local pressure more than made up for it. For whatever reason, cover art after 1955 became steadily more restrained. Perhaps one phase had exhausted itself. Perhaps (in the words of an art director of the period) "cover art just got better." Or perhaps the political pressures were too much, making the trashy paperback in its full flowering another member of the long list of the victims of the Fifties cultural purge, along with the actors, writers, and directors blacklisted for real or alleged left-wing sympathies, the writings of Dr. Wilhelm Reich, and the EC line of horror comics. The world had temporarily been made safe for the *Saturday Evening Post*.

The changes wrought in paperback art were almost universally hailed as being for the better. Frank Schick wrote: "The impact of these various restrictive actions resulted in a toning down of cover art which had previously leaned heavily on magazine type illustration, much of which was actually in bad taste. Since 1953, cover art has followed a new trend stressing abstract design and striking use of typography."

In short, paperbacks had entered the realm of good taste. Along with heaving bosoms and smoking pistols, oil paintings were another casualty of the transition. They did not become extinct, but were increasingly replaced by photography and by pencil or pen-and-ink sketches. The new tendency was typified by Bantam Books. In the words of art director Len Leone (quoted in Clarence Peterson's *The Bantam Story*): "We decided to move the other way. We decided to buy airy, light things. . . . Often when an illustrator would come by with sketches, we liked the lightness and airiness of the sketches and decided to shoot directly from them. Of course, we would pay the full price of a finished painting. This was a constant source of amazement to some of the illustrators."

Cover art ultimately became a kind of logo, an attractive label design. Gone forever was the cinematic palpability which gave one the illusion of peeping through a window at an actual scene. Along with respectability had come sophistication. There was also a new obligatory sense of responsibility: the once tawdry Nanas and Madame Bovarys would take on a demurer mien appropriate to their marketing as Classics rather than as unexpurgated French contraband. It was all very tasteful, very levelheaded, and rather dull. The wild books had been thoroughly domesticated.

Chapter Three

A Disposable Gallery

The art director of a leading paperback publisher glances disdainfully, from across his gleaming Formica desk, at the 1945 title I extend to him. "Frankly," he says, "that art is so bad . . . there's just nothing I can say about it." And the older artists, I inquire, do any of them still do any work for him? "No, you see, those guys were from another era. They wouldn't be able to compete in today's market. With a few exceptions, of course. But the artists today are technically so great, the whole thing has moved to a different level. They are so good it scares me sometimes."

He waves his hand around the room, at next month's cover art, a tumultuous plantation scene overflowing with figures, refined beyond any suggestion of a human hand holding a brush; a hero of the Old West rendered in extraordinarily delicate layers of watercolor—perfection itself. In rapt admiration the art director stands up to examine the canvas in closer detail. "I am constantly amazed. These guys are inventing new techniques. They're in a class with . . . the old masters. They're better than the old masters! In a technical sense. I'm serious. Even the old masters didn't have this kind of precision." He returns to the pile of moldy paperbacks on the desk. "But that stuff? It's crude. It's nothing. They had no sophistication in those days. Whereas today we have the most sophisticated stuff I have ever seen."

I cannot tell him my secret: it is that very crudeness that I have developed an affection for, and even the undeniable perfection of the cover art he has just shown me must be put in a context that somewhat diminishes it. For after all, nowadays everything is perfect: record-album covers, corporate logos, thirty-second television commercials, the type design on cereal boxes, the special effects in science-fiction movies—all have the mark of our era. Clean, precise to a hair's breadth, milky smooth, they seem not so much to have been designed as to have been generated by state-of-the-art technology. Is it coincidental that cover art today, for all its technical inventiveness, suffers from a dearth of ideas and must often resort to recycling the old images? The same old blonde, the same old trenchcoat (and the same old plantation and the same old gunslinger) are played back, camped up, streamlined, mellowed, and glitterized. But it is that old image—and the world it refers to—that provides the emotional juice. Technique is emotionally moving primarily to art directors.

The early paperback covers were anything but state-of-the-art. That pinnacle was represented, for most of the artists, by magazine illustration—above all by the *Saturday Evening Post*, where Norman Rockwell reigned as the court painter of midcentury middle-class America. Working for the paperbacks was a place to start, or a way station on the road to more prestigious assignments. In the meantime, it was a living. Today many of the postwar artists have moved on to other fields (the lucrative market for realistic Western art lured a sizable number of them), and few can look on the work they did for the paperbacks as more than hack work—enjoyable or otherwise, but hardly an accomplishment to boast of.

Of all the things that may be considered when looking at this art, personal style is probably the least significant. A few personal idiosyncrasies stand out, but by and large it is an anonymous medium; indeed, much of the time even the name of the artist is unknown. In those days, just as in the early days of the pulps and the comic books, everything was geared for the moment—it was unthinkable that anyone in the future might care who had executed a particular cover. A paperback was as disposable as a Kleenex, so it is hardly surprising that it was unusual for artists to be credited. There were exceptions: Pocket Books in the

1950s regularly printed the artist's name on the back cover, and Signet covers often bore a recognizable signature. Avon and Popular Library, on the other hand, gave no credit and apparently discouraged artists from signing their work. Of the wonderful series of early Dell mysteries, nearly all are uncredited, although many of the best are now known to be the work of Gerald Gregg.

Finding out who painted a cover is in itself an undertaking that requires detective skills and luck. Tell-tale initials sometimes turn up, hidden as deftly as caricaturist Al Hirschfeld's "Ninas." Sometimes an art director will recognize a style, or even (although it is unlikely) remember the specific assignment. And then there are the artists themselves—if they are alive, and if they can be found, and if they are willing to take credit for work with which they might not any longer care to be associated.

In only forty years, the study of old paperbacks has already become an archaeological matter, and an attempted listing of complete credits for a given publisher is sure to be as full of gaps as a newly uncovered Sumero-Akkadian epic. What you may end up with as chief exhibit is a somewhat tattered old book cover, artist unknown. As for the original painting, the chances are very slim that it will ever turn up. Some originals are in the hand of artists, others have been bought by a small (but growing) band of devoted collectors. Most are long gone, probably lost in some periodic housecleaning at the publisher's offices.

For example, all the paintings commissioned by Popular Library were retained by the publisher until the early 1950s, at which time the artists were contacted and asked if they wanted their pictures back. A few came to pick them up, but the rest didn't bother; consequently, most of the paintings were destroyed. For true collectors, of course, this is not a tragedy but a blessing, since it makes the surviving originals all the rarer.

Yet even with all these lacunae, the quantity of material is daunting. A growing number of collectors' newsletters have for some time been engaged in cataloging the thousands of titles that emanated from Red Circle, Pony, Handi-Books, Comet, and Superior (in addition to more familiar imprints), each title with its own number, of course, and enough bibliographical irregularities—changes of logo, inexplicable departures from format, revisions of cover art to tone down sexual content—to keep an army of researchers busy.

Clearly it would be impossible for a selection of images from this shapeless mass to be anything other than random. In any case, the power conveyed by the covers comes less from the intensity of any single image than from the cumulative effect of hundreds of such images. In the case of individual painters, too, it is usually unrewarding to try to go over their work item by item, looking for occult progressions and transformations. They worked at top speed, with no time to pause over a particularly cherished composition. Even the work of a single artist can encompass hundreds of covers, since the chief criterion of talent at the time was how fast you could churn them out.

The earliest paperback covers derived their manner fairly directly from the dust-cover art of the day. The tone was decorative rather than dramatic, and if the text was respectable enough—the plays of Shakespeare, for instance—even the decorative element might be foregone in favor of a flat, typographically uninteresting cover that simply announced the contents, as if a lack of visual excitement somehow certified the volume's connection to high culture.

Mysteries, on the other hand (and this was a legacy of the previous decade or so of hardcover art), were graced with enigmatic puzzle pictures equivalent to the literary puzzle within. The 1945 Pocket Book edition of S. S. Van Dine's *The Bishop Murder Case* is a typical example. A tiny man walks across a vast chessboard toward a tiny New York City in the distance, while an oversized black pawn dominates the foreground. To the right, a crumbling wall displays a heart-shaped hole, from which a red-feathered arrow shaft protrudes. The anonymous painter has produced what appears at first glance to be a mass-market version of some Dali dreamscape, merely by arranging in very literal fashion the leading clues to the solution of the mystery. (That same year Dali himself would go one step further and produce, for Alfred Hitchcock's *Spellbound*, what seems to be an arty cinematic version of a mass-market-paperback imitation of his own early work, employing the same literal translation of clues into pseudosurrealism.)

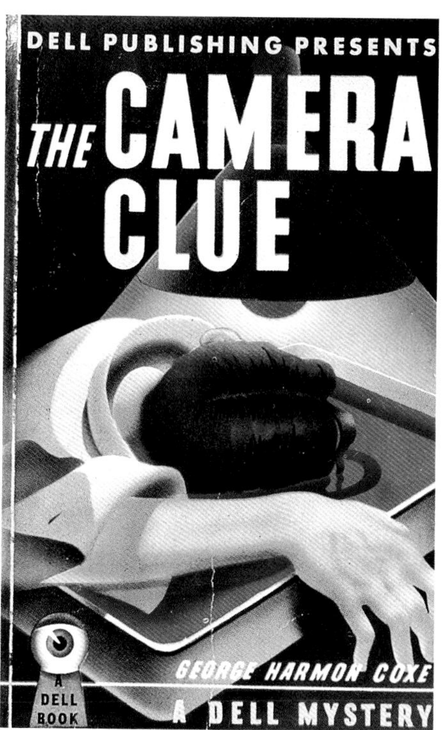

Dell 27 (1943)
Artist: Gerald Gregg

Dell 6 (1943)
Artist: Gerald Gregg

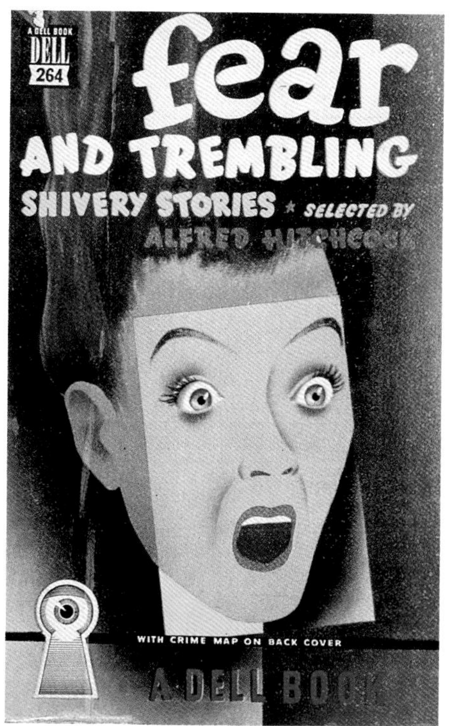

Dell 264 (1948)
Artist: Gerald Gregg

Dell 295 (1949)
Artist: Gerald Gregg

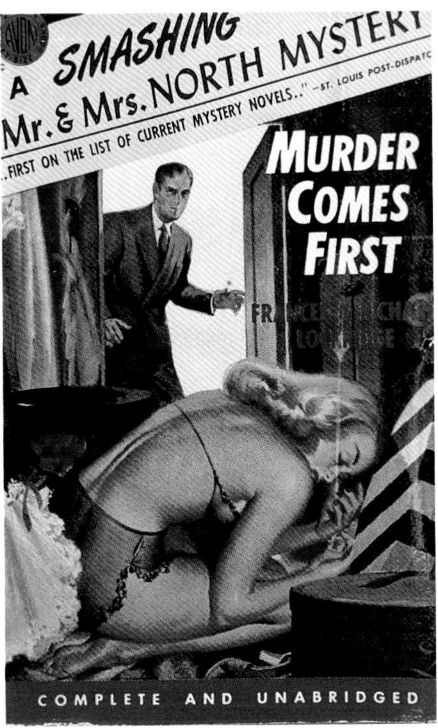

Avon 434 (1952)

Avon 432 (1952)

Avon 258 (1950)

Avon 479 (1952)

Graphic 148 (1957)

Graphic 141 (1956)
Artist: Walter Papp

Graphic 143 (1956)
Artist: Roy Lance

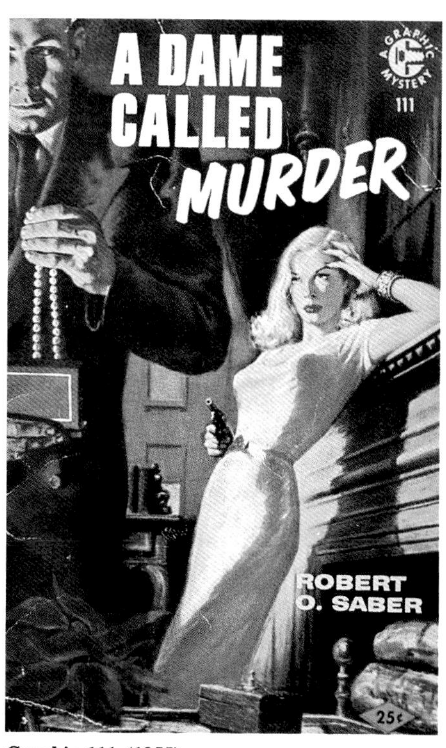

Graphic 111 (1955)
Artist: Walter Papp

Pocket Books 833 (1951)
Artist: Ray App

Graphic 81 (1963)

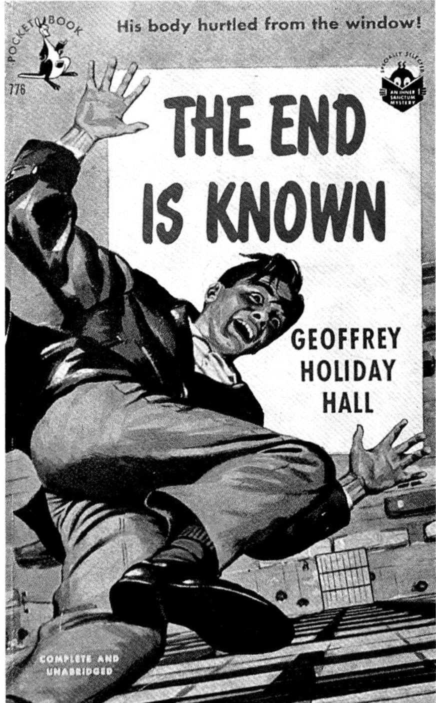

Pocket Books 776 (1951)
Artist: Paul Kresse

Handi-Books 134 (1951)
Artist: Norman Saunders

Popular Library 382 (1951)
Artist: Rudolph Belarski

Popular Library 310 (1951)

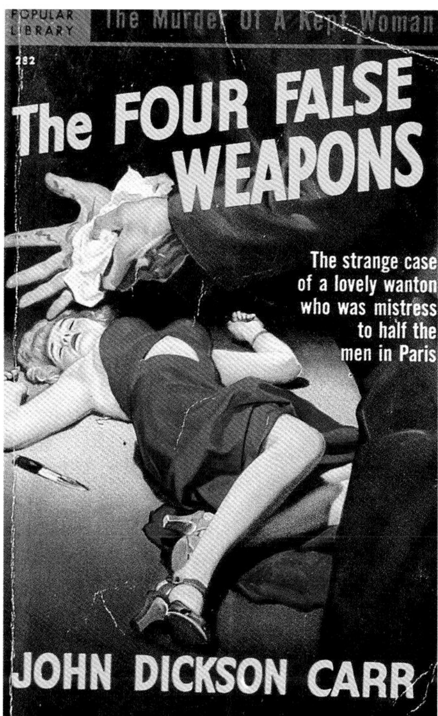

Popular Library 282 (1950)
Artist: Rudolph Belarski

Popular Library 218 (1949)
Artist: Rudlph Belarski

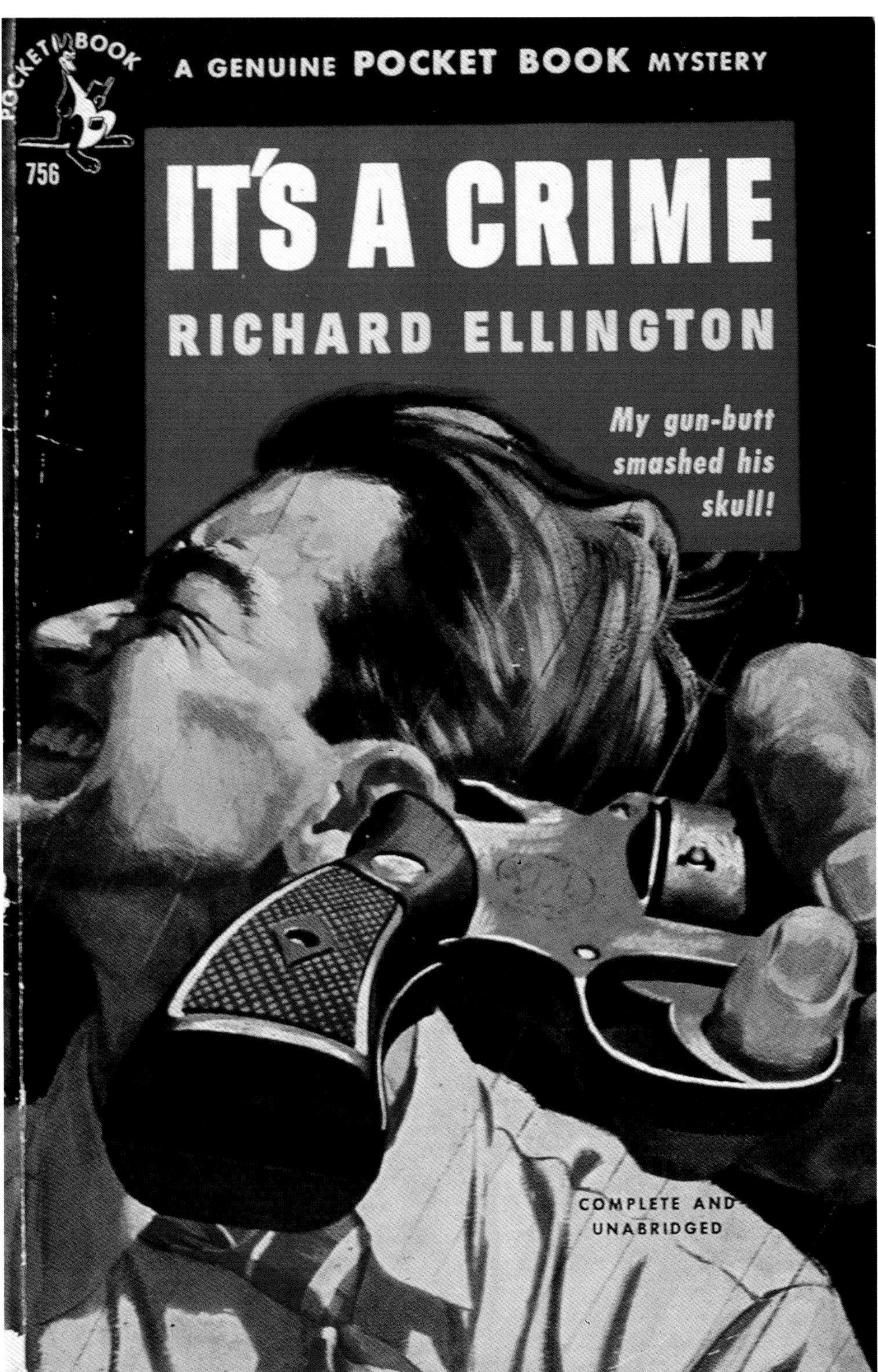

Pocket Books 756 (1951)
Artist: Paul Kresse

Signet 937 (1952)
Artist: James Avati

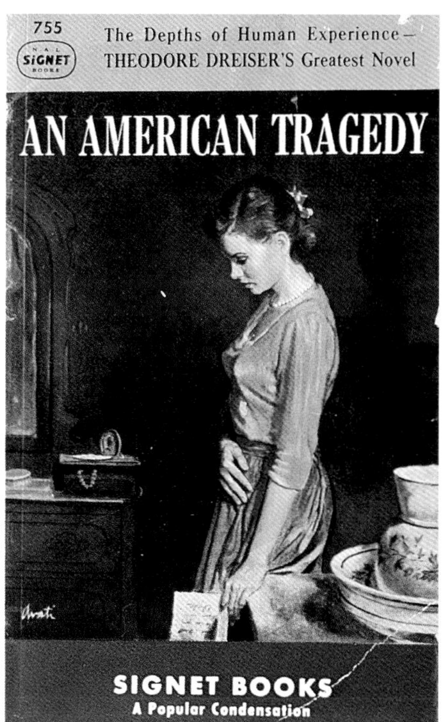

Signet 755 (1949)
Artist: James Avati

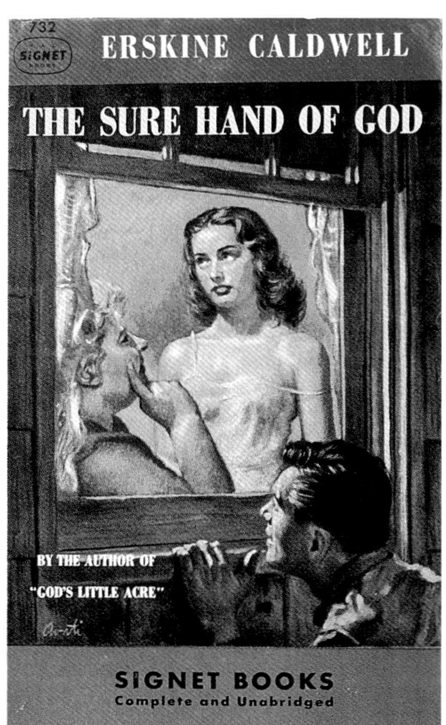

Signet 732 (1949)
Artist: James Avati

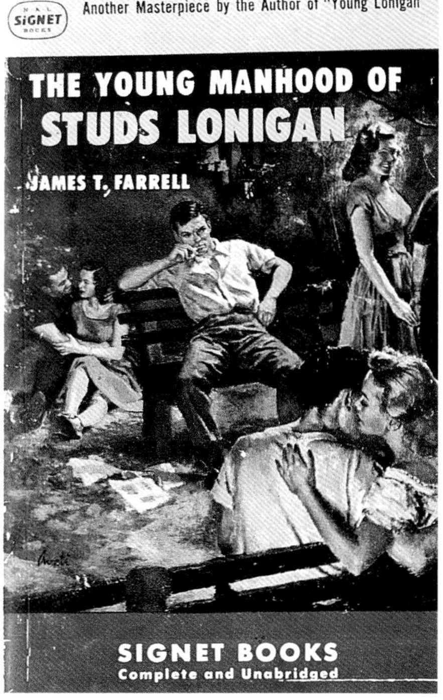

Signet 810 (1950)
Artist: James Avati

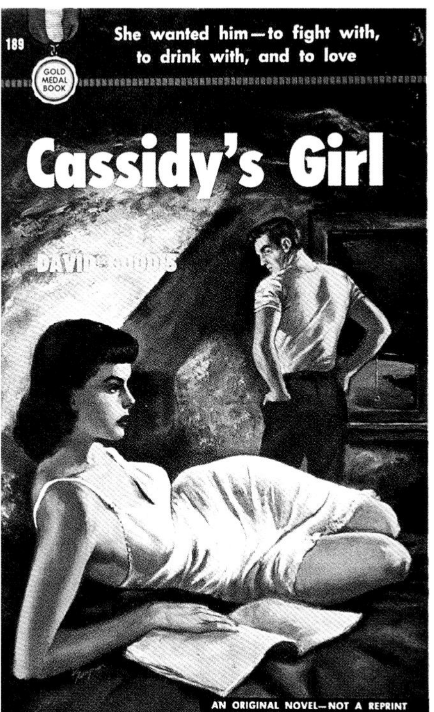

Gold Medal 189 (1951)

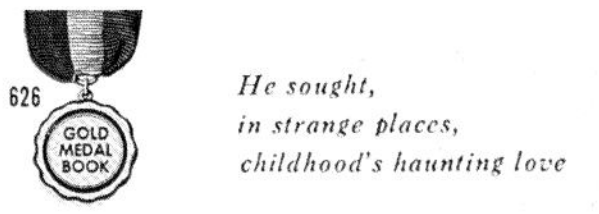

Gold Medal 626 (1956)
Artist: Barye Phillips

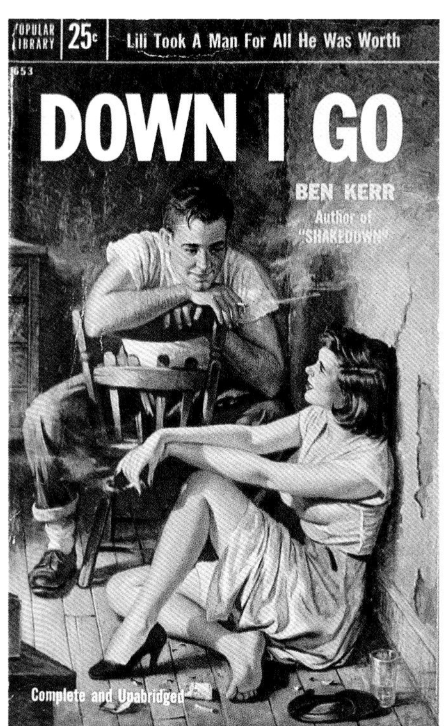

Popular Library 653 (1955)

Popular Library 528 (1953)

Pocket Books 138 (1942)
Artist: Pierre Martinot

Pocket Books 305 (1945)

Pocket Books 248 (1944)
Artist: Leo Manso

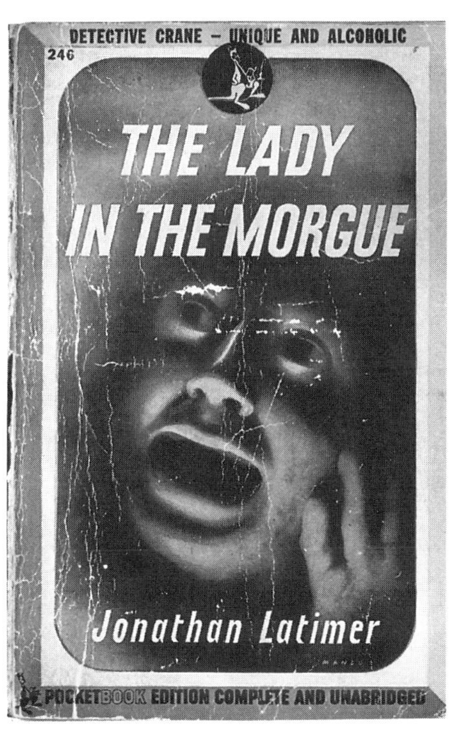

Pocket Books 246 (1944)
Artist: Leo Manso

Pocket's early mystery covers mostly conveyed an impression of mysteries as harmless, formalist structures. The cat ("Sorry about that cat on the cover," said the cover copy. "Should have been a gray Persian, but he turned out to be a Siamese. Rebuke to our art editor.") that stalks the 1942 edition of Erle Stanley Gardner's *The Case of the Caretaker's Cat* is an emblem of menace, but it is unlikely to arouse any real sense of danger, only a comforting awareness of precisely the kind of predictable pleasures to be found within. Again, the 1945 cover for Raymond Chandler's *The High Window* features what was to become a familiar motif, that of a person falling from a window; but the body is a tiny black figure against a few stylized (and very crudely drawn) buildings. Thus, we register the fact that a person is falling, but feel none of the sense of horror that would attend the actuality. In contrast, Norman Saunders' 1951 painting (for Handi-Books' *Murder Is Dangerous*) of a man falling from an oil derrick gives us the face in closeup, the hands grasping air, the rolling eyes, and, centrally, the mouth that screams. We are forced to contemplate, if only for a second, the emotions of a victim who will remain otherwise unknown to us unless we accept the invitation to buy the book.

The most distinctive artist to work for Pocket Books in the pre-1945 period was Leo Manso, who specialized in mysteries and produced work that ranged from the purely formal to something closer to the emotionally charged postwar art. At his most formal the result is fairly bland, as in the 1944 edition of *The Maltese Falcon*, where three not very excited-looking hands grope in the direction of the black bird, displayed against a nebulous orange background. We can see why in 1951 Pocket (or rather its subsidiary Perma) chose to use in its place a considerably more provocative painting by Stanley Meltzoff. However inappropriate the erotic suggestion of Meltzoff's cover, it is infinitely more dramatic than the Manso collage effect.

Nevertheless, Manso did come up with some memorable covers, such as the 1943 *Glass Key*, with its two trench-coated, slouch-hatted figures confronting each other against a featureless night sky. It has something of the calm and colorless paranoia of a Fritz Lang film. It is in fact, with Lang's work and Graham Greene's novels, a perfect product of its period: hero and villain are indistinguishable—a confusion entirely fit-

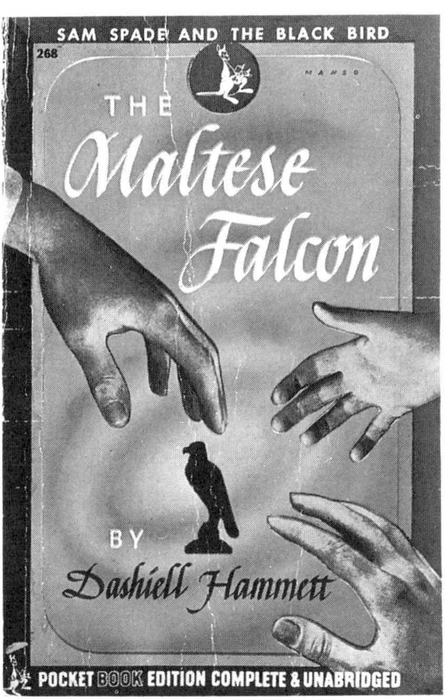

Pocket Books 268 (1944)
Artist: Leo Manso

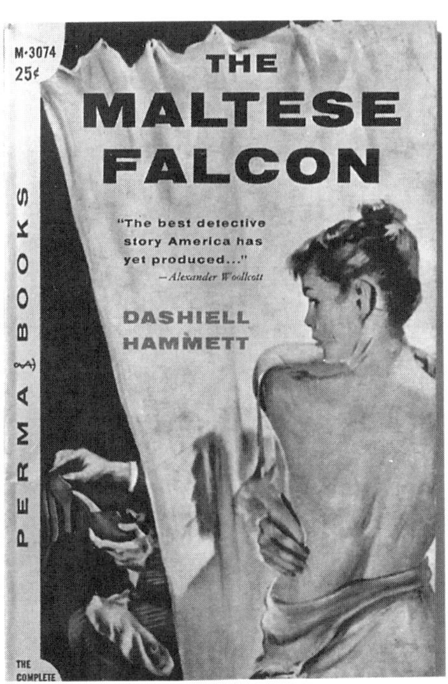

Perma M3074 (1957)
Artist: Stanley Meltzoff

ting, considering the ambiguity of Hammett's text. The draftsmanship is far more stylized than would be the norm after the war. The cover is still an emblem, not yet a peep through a window. The tormented faces Manso painted for *The Lady in the Morgue* and *The Canary Murder Case* (both 1944) emerge from a blurred or empty background. The discolored skin and unnatural lighting of the screaming face that adorns the first book has an effect perhaps slightly more horrific than intended, and certainly more anguished than Latimer's knock-about comedy warranted. Similarly, the cover for the Van Dine novel emphasizes physical brutality—in safely stylized form—to a degree that the fastidious creator of Philo Vance might well have considered distasteful. Nevertheless, compared with the blatant sexualization of murder that became a standard procedure in the following decade, Manso's cover is very mild.

Whatever their deficiencies, the early Pocket covers seem triumphs of design compared with their counterparts at Avon. As was noted in the previous chapter, Avon took its aesthetic lead from the pulps, but the artists they employed lacked the technical proficiency of the best pulp illustrators. In the postwar years, Avon's covers would improve slightly, but in a rather anachronistic way; an Avon cover from 1943 looks like a very bad pulp cover, while an Avon cover from 1951 looks like a reasonably good pulp cover. Only very rarely did Avon attempt an artistic flourish such as the blonde death's head surrounded by orchids on the 1943 edition of *The Big Sleep*, another example of the symbolic school of mystery illustration.

Far more appealing were the books that Dell began to publish in 1943. At its outset Dell was associated almost exclusively with mysteries, and adopted as a marketing tactic a unique design that has made its early titles the most widely collected of paperbacks. In fact, the New York-based company served primarily as distributor for the books, which were designed and printed in Wisconsin by Western Printing and Lithographing Company. Unfortunately, the artists were given no credit, although the researches of paperback historian William Lyles revealed the importance of staff painter Gerald Gregg, whose style typifies the Dell look, with its vibrant blocks of color and seamless airbrushed edges. "According to Gregg," wrote Lyles, "the airbrush lets the artist paint with soft lines, giving the pictures a soft, full and flowing quality."

The Dell books were outstanding for their elaborate gimmickry. The trademark was an eyeball staring through a keyhole, and nearly every book had a brightly colored map on the back, which presumably enabled the pedantically inclined reader to actually follow the characters' peregrinations through the gardens and studies and greenhouses and old towers of each and every whodunit. The artwork of the maps bore a strong resemblance to the board of the game Clue, with its neat little rectangular rooms, stocked with tables, lamps, sofas, desks, and dressers, but with never a person or indeed any trace of personality in its furnishings.

If the maps were not enough, Dell provided as many as four appetite-whetting pages of interior copy to lure the reader into the precincts of the book itself. First one was introduced to "Persons this *Mystery* is about," persons like "JENNY THORNE, dark-haired and lovely, has slightly Oriental eyes which give her the look of a startled faun . . . But because of the nameless fear which has darkened her whole life, she is almost afraid of her own happiness" or "CHARLES CUSHMAN, tough ex-chief of detectives, operates a plushy gambling joint and he is either doing all right by himself or he will soon be a lavishly equipped bankruptcy." Next followed an equally tantalizing list of "*Things* this Mystery is about": "Two exposed PHOTOGRAPHIC PLATES . . . An initialed COMPACT . . . A used highball GLASS . . . A package of indiscreet LETTERS . . . CLIPPINGS from a gossip column . . . A gigantic SANDWICH MAN . . . Bullet HOLES in a wall . . . A much-wanted PICTURE." These catalogs of objects sometimes attained an unexpectedly poetic tone.

If the reader was still not hooked, there remained the ultimate question: "Wouldn't You Like To Know—How a man with no reason for disappearing could vanish for seven years? What Dragon's Blood is? What it is used for? Why it is not hard to shoot a gun from a man's hand? Who was the naked person that brushed by Mary in the black night? What blood-curdling sight caused Wallace's perpetual neurotic stammer? How to trick an innocent person into killing himself? What really happened on that terrible day which haunts two families for a generation? Why Gail Proctor suddenly took to locking her bedroom door? What anyone would want with a pair of dead hands?"

They are a small-scale demonstration of the book as toy. (The larger-scale version would be those late Thirties CrimeFile volumes where you got the actual pieces of evidence—cartridges, partly burned letters, stray hairs—and had to plow your way through carbon copies of affidavits in order to work out the mystery.) The covers, in keeping with that spirit, emphasized objects and places rather than people. Such people as did appear tended to be made grotesque, although it was a harmless grotesqueness, the grotesqueness of a Halloween mask looming among all the other bold-colored, soft-edged objects: a red-tinged icepick; an enormous microscope under whose lens a Lilliputian corpse lies prostrate; a green, fanged demon face grinning atop a blue-faced victim; a limp body hanging chained from a police badge.

Most memorably, on one of the earliest Dell covers, there was a pastoral landscape of rolling hills and cloud-covered moon, all softened by the ubiquitous airbrush, and in its midst a red lake. The red, as always, is symbolic of blood: but it is all too lovely to partake of real gore. It

Dell 264 (1948) (back cover)

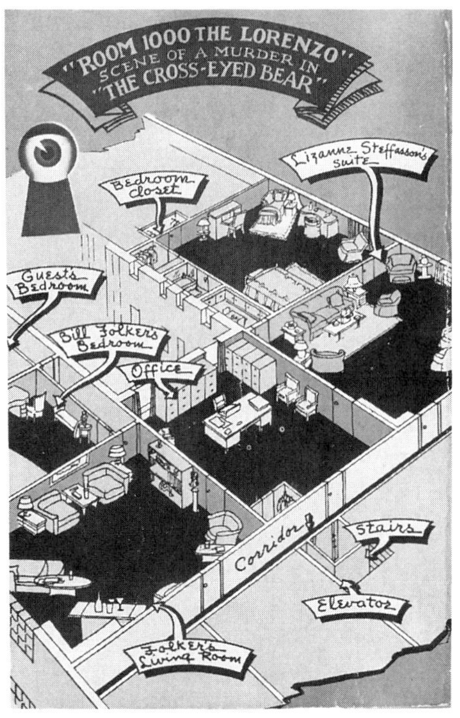

Dell 48 (back cover)

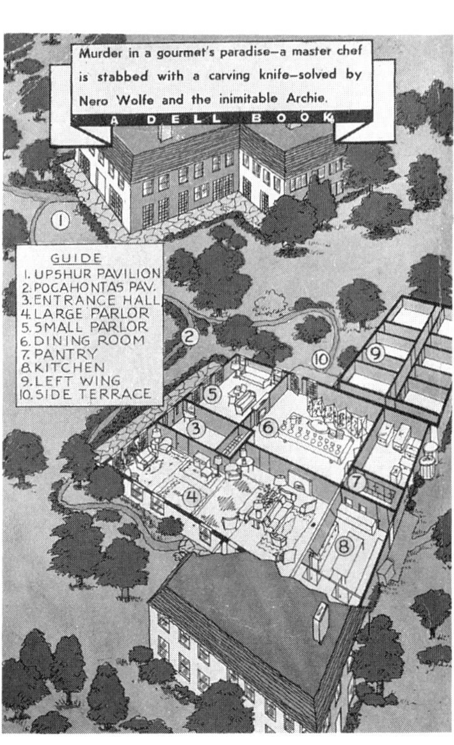

Dell 540 (back cover)

Dell 46 (back cover)

Dell 452 (back cover)

is Agatha Christie adapted by Walt Disney, a cozy and thrilling poster art that has—somehow, somewhere, remotely—a connection with death and horror. They were by far the most imaginative of the early paperbacks.

The war years produced that art, just as they produced the monumentally delicate textures of Glenn Miller's greatest hits and Carmen Miranda's psychedelic Technicolor bananas in *The Gang's All Here*. The postwar period in its deflation of thenceforth useless morale-building escapism, gave birth to something quite different.

Stanley Meltzoff, whose covers appeared on numerous Signet and Pocket titles in the postwar years, recalls that "the art directors thought it was their covers that were selling the books. But the real reason people bought books was that they wanted to read." Pocket Books had purveyed the high culture of Shakespeare and Jane Austen, and the wide culture of *Mrs. Miniver* and *Random Harvest*, but had carefully steered clear of anything too modern or too frank or too intellectual. Avon filled the gap to some extent with Ben Hecht, Noel Coward, and even a little D. H. Lawrence, but for the real stuff of modern literature and ideas the source was New American Library, the former American branch of Penguin Books which had gone independent in 1949.

NAL's titles appeared under two imprints. Mentor Books ("Good Reading for the Millions") featured titles of a seriousness unprecedented in the paperback format: Freud, Alfred North Whitehead, Bertrand Russell, Margaret Mead, Suzanne K. Langer, Thorstein Veblen. In effect they provided the intellectual curriculum for a hitherto untapped audience that had nowhere else to turn for such material at that price. Mentor Books became an institution on the order of television's *Omnibus*, and could stand as the paperback industry's lone defense against charges of rampant exploitation. The imprint was without question the most accessible repository of general ideas in America at the time.

Mentor knew its limits. It would offer Schweitzer sooner than Sartre, and would restrict its leftism to an R. H. Tawney or a Sidney Webb rather than venture into the wilds of revolutionary thought (at any rate without a suitably moderate guide to keep things under control). All in all, Mentor represented a benign liberalism and a somewhat naive trust in the power of good books to lead humanity into the light. But given the intellectual climate of the Fifties, Mentor did its job well and exercised an influence over several generations, an influence that faded only with the advent of more adventurous, academically oriented paperback imprints such as Anchor, Meridian, and Vintage.

Mentor's covers had a uniform look owing largely to the fact that they were mostly the work of a single artist—Robert Jonas—whose abstract collages and stylized paintings are familiar to anyone who recalls the Mentor editions of *Patterns of Culture*, *Growing Up in New Guinea*, *Man in the Modern World*, *Philosophy in a New Key*, and literally hundreds of other titles.

Mentor was an outgrowth of the Pelican imprint's American branch; the Penguin line itself evolved into Signet Books. In fact, the American Penguins bore little resemblance to their English counterparts. The austere color-coded covers (green for mysteries, blue for belles lettres) were replaced by paintings (many of them also by Jonas) notable for bright colors and a relatively modernist style. They managed to suggest some buoyant pleasure to be found in Modern Literature while definitely preserving a more genteel tone than their more raucous competitors.

American Penguin's list went easy on British authors (limiting itself to figures of the stature of Shaw or Maugham) while playing up the American angle. William Faulkner, James T. Farrell, John Dos Passos, Erskine Caldwell, James M. Cain, Richard Wright, John O'Hara—all were represented, betraying a strong penchant in the editorial department for the mainstream of American realism.

After the transition to Signet, the list expanded to include hundreds of current novelists, many of them offering visions quite radical by the standards of the day: Paul Bowles (*The Sheltering Sky*), Chester Himes (*If He Hollers Let Him Go*), Vladimir Nabokov (*Laughter in the Dark*), Gore Vidal (*The City and the Pillar*), Alberto Moravia (*The Woman of Rome*), Chandler Brossard (*Who Walk In Darkness*) became mass-market authors alongside Robert Heinlein, Howard Hunt, Ayn Rand, and Mickey Spillane. Perhaps the most influential of all Signet's titles was

George Orwell's *1984*, which, sold under the guise of a sexy science-fiction novel, was internalized by a whole generation of young readers.

Concurrently with its change of name, Signet's cover art moved rapidly from stylization to realism. By about 1948, a new look had taken over the industry. Abstraction was out; the demand now was for pictures so real that they looked as if they would reach out and touch you, pictures detailed enough to appear like a peep through a forbidden window. How real this realism was depended to some extent on the publisher and to some extent on the draftsmanship of the artist. Rudolph Belarski, for instance, had already had a long career painting covers for pulps like *Wings*, *Round-Up*, and *Phantom Detective*. He provided for Popular Library a series of covers notable for a realism utterly divorced from reality, in which women of unlikely proportions and oddly glowing flesh were featured as either perpetrators or victims: brandishing automatics, cowering (on white fur rugs) from revolvers, or lying murdered in red silk gowns, all without ever disturbing their elaborate coiffures. Belarski and his publishers were far more involved with textures of hair and skin and fabric than with dramatic tension.

By the mid-1950s, Popular Library had changed its look. Although the fixation on women's breasts remained constant, the glossiness had given way to a grainier tone, in keeping with the new democratization of subject matter that was by then in full swing. A novel was more likely to concern a murderous gas station attendant than a murderous baroness. Ray Johnson's 1955 covers for John D. MacDonald's *Cry Hard, Cry Fast* and Jim Thompson's *After Dark, My Sweet* are, if fantasies, distinctly localized fantasies, with something of a specific time and place attaching to them, unlike the gaudy boudoirs of Belarski's Neverland. The stylistic change that took place in the period from 1947 to 1955 had to do with the declining appeal of a glamour that had lost much of its power to enchant, and, as the older dream faded, the emergence of a more unblinking contemplation of the surfaces of the world.

The same process took place within every publishing house, not always with happy results. By 1948, Dell had switched to relatively realistic effects, dropping once and for all the brilliant poster style of the war years. Unfortunately, the later covers never really found a style, and must be counted among the least interesting of the Fifties. They lacked even the trashiness that might have given them some intensity of the kind that abounds in the product of publishers like Ace, Handi-Books, and Graphic. These lower-echelon houses were what people had in mind when they spoke of "trashy paperbacks." These were books that virtually guaranteed (by the clear-cut standards of 1954, at any rate) an absence of any redeeming value, literary, social, or otherwise. They made that guarantee by means of incredibly atmospheric covers such as those by Walter Papp, in which a Veronica Lake type leans a braceleted arm against the mantelpiece while aiming a pistol at a Paul Stewart type who holds a string of pearls in his hand (*A Dame Called Murder*); or the smoky den of vice in which nearly every object present—cocktail glass, bracelet, cigarette, bulging trenchcoat, oversized cufflink—is intended to convey an impression of steamy corruption (*Dressed to Kill*).

They make their impression through an utter lack of hesitation, a certainty of intent that makes a direct impact. Other, more straightlaced publishers cultivated a more ambiguous tone, one that would enable them to work both sides of the street. Bantam, which had begun publishing in 1945, staked out a middle-of-the-road position, offering both *The Great Gatsby* and *Guns from Powder Valley*, *A Bell for Adano* and *Date with Death*. The artwork was more individualized than that of other publishers; Bantam even included a little note about the cover, often just a sample of the relevant portion of the text ("Then she suddenly screamed, 'Don't! Oh, God, don't, don't!'"), but sometimes adding a comment on the artist ("After shivering and shuddering through this unusual novel of suspense and passion, artist William Shoyer painted that woman, Clara Ervin, posing luxuriously in her pink satin boudoir. As for the man in the cover who is beholding her at a close and menacing range, you'll find out what happens next when you enjoy BEHOLD THIS WOMAN").

The Bantam covers featured work by artists like Tom Lovell and Ken Riley, who were notable for their technical ability, if not necessarily for the emotional impact of their covers; but then, in the world of paperbacks, emotion and technique do not always go together. The maga-

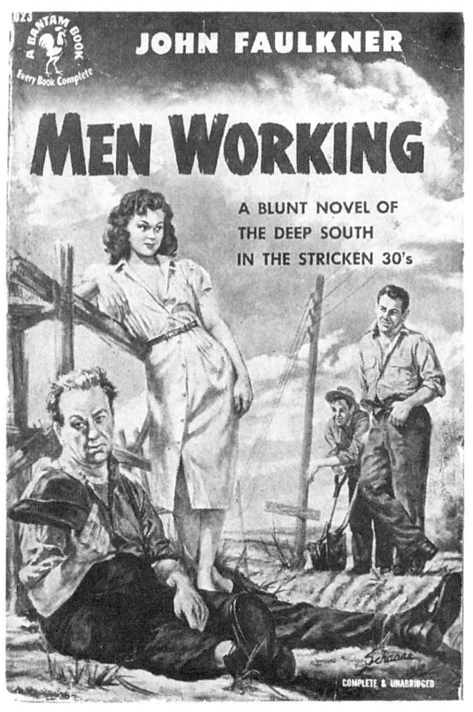

Bantam 1023 (1952)
Artist: Harry Schaare

Bantam 1026 (1952)

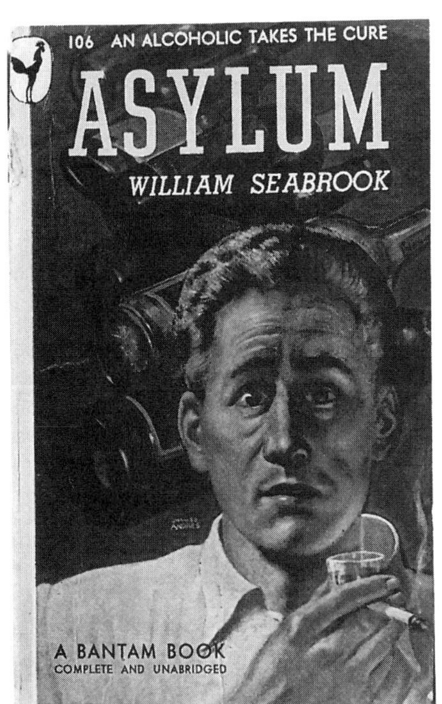

Bantam 106 (1947)
Artist: Charles Andres

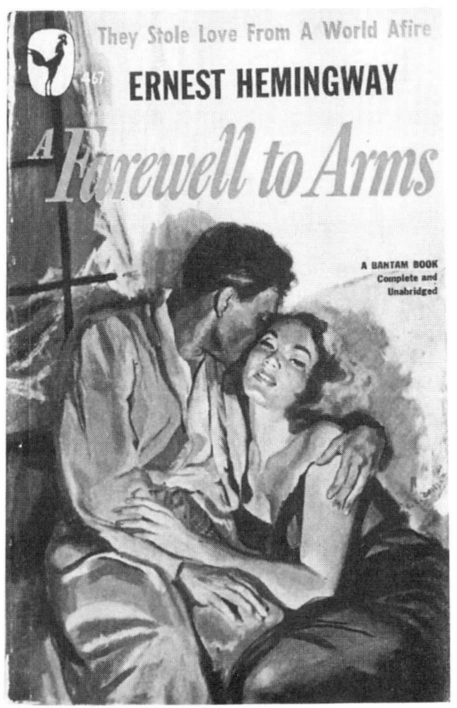

Bantam 467 (1948)
Artist: C. C. Beall

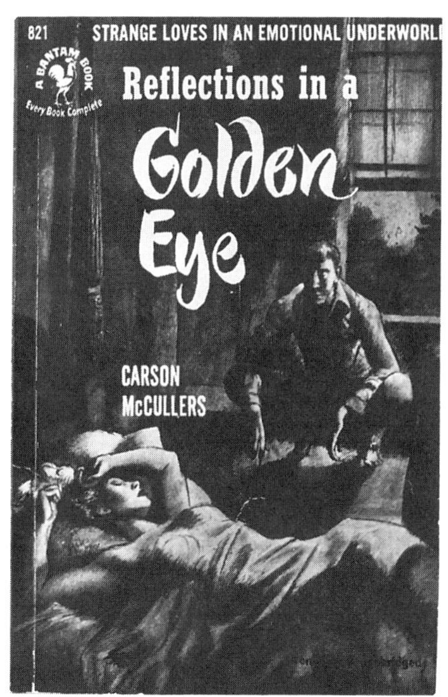

Bantam 821 (1949)

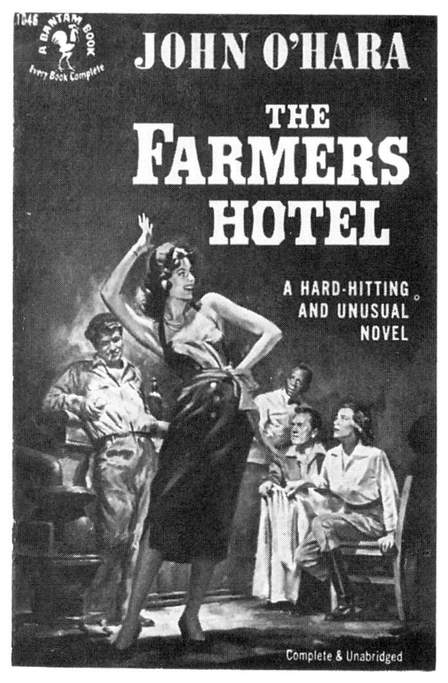

Bantam 1046 (1952)
Artist: Michael Hooks

zine-style paintings done by Lovell for Maugham's *Stranger in Paris* (a.k.a. *Christmas Holiday*) and by C. C. Beall for Hemingway's *A Farewell to Arms* are nicely textured but static, while William Shoyer's above-mentioned cover for *Behold This Woman* is far cruder but considerably more potent.

Bantam occasionally struck a more prestigious note if the material warranted it. For Steinbeck's *The Wayward Bus*, "Ben Stahl, master artist, who also did the cover for Bantam's edition of *Cannery Row*, again captures in color and line the innermost emotions of two turbulent Steinbeck characters," and the uncredited artist who did the very effective cover for Carson McCullers' *Reflections in a Golden Eye* aimed for a style reminiscent of Reginald Marsh. But these had little to do with the mainstream of paperback art, any more than did Signet's atypical covers by Reginald Marsh (*Tobacco Road*) and Thomas Hart Benton (*A Streetcar Named Desire*). The best of Bantam was represented by a certain homely realism typified by Harry Schaare's *Men Working* cover and by Mitchell Hooks' painting for *The Farmers Hotel*.

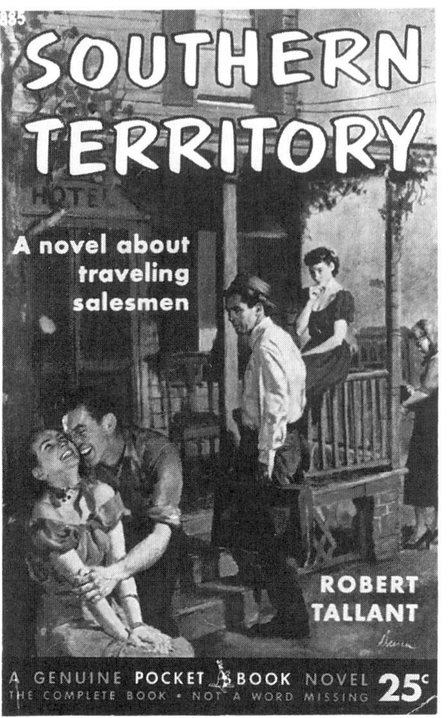

Pocket Books 885 (1952)
Artist: Tom Dunn

Pocket Books 878 (1952)
Artist: Tom Dunn

Perma M3061 (1956)
Artist: Lou Marchetti

Pocket Books/Cardinal C-144 (1954)
Artist: Tom Dunn

Signet 1152 (1955)
Artist: Stanley Zuckerberg

Signet 1107 (1954)
Artist: Stanley Zuckerberg

Signet 714 (1949)
Artist: James Avati

Signet 760 (1949)
Artist: James Avati

Pocket Books also revamped its style, imparting a new toughness to its Chandler and Hammett titles and proving in general that it was fully capable of meeting the challenge from competitors who were by now springing up on all sides. Pocket's artists included many highly competent craftsmen—James Meese, Robert Schulz, Stanley Meltzoff, Lou Marchetti, Clark Hulings, Frank McCarthy, Paul Kresse, and the prolific Tom Dunn—whose collective work made Pocket (and its offshoot Perma) in effect the most typical paperback house of the Fifties, as it had been of the Forties. The most famous single image it produced was probably Clark Hulings' painting for *The Blackboard Jungle* (1955), in which a T-shirted punk tests the edge of his switchblade while gazing obliquely at the reader, some nameless blend of resentment and amused anticipation playing about his face.

But the culmination of the postwar style was the brand of realism explored by New American Library from 1949 until the mid-1950s. James Avati—almost universally considered by his peers as the finest paperback artist of that period—succeeded in tempering the prevalent luridness of paperback art with a sober realism that was all the more effective for its relative restraint. Whereas most publishers were content that every book should look nearly the same as the rest—a few tumultuous figures flaunting flesh and gunsmoke for a quick kill at the newsstand—Avati and other painters like Stanley Zuckerberg and James Meese focused on the specific subject matter of the work they were illustrating, and filled out the little world on the book cover with a full, richly observed background. The solidity of the location made the action depicted more real.

The overall design of Signet covers helped. The paintings were set off in a frame, and the typography gave the art room to breathe. It was the old idea of looking through a window, but for once what you saw when you looked through was actually unexpected. That singularity is the most striking aspect of James Avati's covers. Each is a conscious summation of the book it illustrates (and it appears that Avati, unlike many artists, actually *read* the books). This was appropriate for New American Library, which was in the business of selling individual titles rather than a mass of indistinguishable product. Each book needed its own signature. This Avati accomplished—so well that for many readers his images inevitably rise to memory when they think of, say, *Invisible Man* or *The Woman of Rome*.

His emphasis was usually on character more than incident. We get a series of portraits—for instance, the spare medium shot of the unfortunate Roberta in *An American Tragedy*, a painting that manages to live up to the cover copy's promise of "The Depths of Human Experience." It does this by eliminating all external action or passion, confronting us with just a girl looking downward, a letter from her lover in her left hand while her right rests lightly on her belly (a discreet acknowledgment of pregnancy), against a bare brown wall, an old-fashioned bureau flush against it, and in the foreground, on the cheap table, the jug and washbowl with their delicate and precisely noted pattern of birds and branches. This depiction of emptiness and deprivation dates from 1949, the year Avati began painting covers.

On the other hand, we have Christopher Isherwood's Sally Bowles on the 1952 edition of *Goodbye to Berlin*, a portrait of provocation, with her high heels, long cigarette holder, green fingernails, and short yellow skirt, her seductive oddly awkward pose, and beyond that first impression the tatty sofa, the stained wall, the picture hanging awry, the articles of clothing strewn about the room, the hairbrush and gold lipstick case and bits of silk piled on the gracefully curved night table. The publishers call this "Bohemian Life in a Wicked City," and it is all that—Avati created a whole world of European interiors for postwar Americans. But more astonishingly, it allows us, if we choose, to see a real person in such clothes and such a room, rather than simply the standard icon of The Seductress. By allowing us that little margin of choice, it is quietly undermining mental and moral structures built up over many decades. It is implying that Bohemians are in fact flesh-and-blood creatures and that wickedness is just a word, not to be compared in its impact to actualities of wood and cloth and smoke and flesh and mind.

Signet had found the exact midpoint of American culture, and had staked out its position there. Whatever contradiction existed between high and low, between literature and exploitation, were to be welded together in a single image. It is the blending of opposite points of view that gives the Signet covers their vitality. At first glance the artwork seems part of the usual trashy paperback syndrome. But when you look again, the setting comes into focus, the faces are seen to have ambiguous expressions, the instant reading of the pulp cover has given way to something unsettled and quietly disturbing. The composition is objective, and therefore powerful. It is also designed to sustain a multitude of interpretations, to offer something different to each point of view.

In cruder terms, it's a kind of double game. For instance, is Vasco Pratolini's *The Naked Streets* a serious literary work by "one of the most successful and important literary figures in postwar Italy," or is it a haven for thrill seekers? Signet very neatly has it both ways. On the one hand, we have a blurb from *The Nation* and a reference to the "need to find some lasting meaning in life and love." On the other hand, we are promised a gallery of characters who are "impatient to explore love" and "teasing and provocative," "the fiery Marisa" and "the beautiful young Olga." Stanley Zuckerberg's cover painting expertly treads the thin line. There is a young girl attractive enough to qualify for the paperback market, but with a pale complexion and dour expression that undercut the sex angle. Four young hoods swagger at a street corner, conjuring up *The Amboy Dukes* or *The Blackboard Jungle*, but at the same time we have another shabbily dressed youth whose painful sensitivity is obvious at a glance. What holds it together is the narrow-laned Italian slum crisscrossed with washing, which asserts that this is a real scene happening in a real place.

Such a painting is, among other things, a triumph of format, of suggesting within the small dimensions of a book cover a larger world that one could walk through. Taken together, the Signet covers present something like a twentieth-century equivalent of Currier and Ives: a succession of park benches, diners, tenement hallways, deserted boarding houses, backwoods shanties, and, for variety, uneasy suburban cocktail parties, all preserved for us; by contrast, the logo-like paperback art of the Seventies left us little to remember but a supermarket full of demons and giant sharks.

What surprises in the end is how much of the paperback art of the Forties and Fifties conveys a sense of reality and a warmth of emotion. Even the fantasies have a homespun texture, and the most unreal of them are brought down to earth, if only by the crudeness of their exe-

1061

The Heartaches and Triumphs of Youth in Love

The Naked Streets

VASCO
PRATOLINI

A SIGNET BOOK
Complete and Unabridged

Signet 1061 (1953)
Artist: Stanley Zuckerberg

Signet 1185 (1955)
Artist: Stanley Zuckerberg

Signet 1138 (1954)
Artist: James Meese

Signet S1624 (1959)
Artist: James Avati

Signet 1033 (1953)
Artist: James Meese

cution. Today's spell-casters have more elaborate tools at their disposal for imparting a magical aura to the ever more efficient packaging. The success story of the media has culminated in a kind of computerized aesthetics not programmed for loose ends, in which considerations like corporate identity and demographics are part of every image. When the bright lights and synthesized soundtracks of today's conglomerate marketing merge into a single vast blur, it is comforting to rest a while in the clear lines of the ramshackle porch on the cover of Erskine Caldwell's *Journeyman*, or to sit with Studs Lonigan in the park on a warm summer night. In retrospect, it is hard to believe that such simplicity once sold books.

Chapter Four

Mythologists of the Hardboiled

The innermost kernel of the paperback was naturally the text itself. At least in theory, the outer display stemmed from this source, although the link was not always obvious. The fictional tradition was the ultimate treasure house of images, no matter how they might be transformed by the shifting expediencies of fashion. The covers were largely illustrations of that body of literature, in the same sense that Medieval art might be said to consist of illustrations of the Bible, and much Renaissance and Baroque art of illustrations of classical mythology.

The hardboiled literature on which the paperbacks thrived and to which they ultimately contributed partook, in its heart, of a demonic vision. Publishers often tried to make that vision more ribald and colorful than the original texts warranted. After all, the public wanted gunfights and Lana Turner, not existentialism and *l'acte gratuit*.

The texts in question can be dated for convenience from 1922, when Dashiell Hammett published his first *Black Mask* story. Other progenitors could be (and have been) invoked: Ernest Hemingway (whom just about everybody eventually tried to imitate), Gertrude Stein (whom Hemingway in turn had imitated, and who would make an interesting creation goddess for the hardboiled detective story, a genre she enjoyed so much that she insisted on meeting Dashiell Hammett on her celebrated American tour of the mid-'30s), or Mark Twain (who had made the first determined effort to write in the American language). Stylistically they are all relevant. As far as content goes, one could trace the elements of noir and hardboiled fiction back through that gothic strain which runs like a crack down the middle of American literature, from Charles Brockden Brown's *Wieland* to Herman Melville's *Pierre, or The Ambiguities*. What Hammett did of special note was to wed a style to a brutally mechanized and updated version of that mythology. The result was a specifically modern demonology.

Demons had been around in America since the beginning, infesting the backwoods settlements of Charles Brockden Brown and the imagined European castles of Edgar Allan Poe, the Indian camps of James Fenimore Cooper and the New England villages of Nathaniel Hawthorne, not to mention all the spaces—ship's holds and South Sea islands, Hudson Valley landholdings and Mississippi steamboats—in which the imagination of Herman Melville went wandering. But it wasn't until Hammett that the demons rode on the municipal bus and rented rooms in cheap hotels. Something clicked: it was "realism," the realest yet. Yet beyond the lifelike shimmering of the surface, something else showed through, the lineaments of a dream or of a primal epic.

The realist element was far from negligible. Following Hammett's lead, the crime novel became a major vehicle for social analysis. Even allowing for generous doses of fantasy and melodrama, it is possible to get a coherent picture of the underside of American life from the works of Hammett, James M. Cain, Raymond Chandler, Horace McCoy, David Goodis, Ross Macdonald, John D. MacDonald, and such latter-day practitioners as George V. Higgins, Donald Westlake, and Elmore Leonard. This phenomenon is more remarkable if you consider that although the detective novel has flourished for over a century in England, it is only very recently (thanks to the likes of Ruth Rendell and P. D. James) that its practitioners have conveyed much impression of British society beyond the upper echelons.

Hammett was in every way the pivotal writer. Raymond Chandler, in "The Simple Art of Murder," wrote of him: "Hammett gave murder back to the kind of people that commit it for reasons, not just to provide a corpse. . . . He put these people down on paper as they are, and he made them talk and think in the language they customarily used for these purposes . . . And he demonstrated that the detective story can be important writing."

The hardboiled novel was born complete in *Red Harvest* in 1929, after a decade of experiments in the pages of *Black Mask*. The contemporary style which Hammett invented in the Twenties stayed contemporary, despite changing argot and a changing society, through the Thirties, Forties, and Fifties. As late as 1952 (before the anti-Communist crusaders brought his name into disrepute), Hammett's old magazine stories were still being dredged up and issued as if new; and his influence as a writer remained vital, even though his last novel had been published in 1934. When I first read *Red Harvest* in 1968, it impressed me not as a museum piece but as a remarkably original and brilliant exercise in the American language, and considering the tenacity with which it remains in print, it appears to have preserved that freshness for others as well.

Hammett's impact has been attributed to his realism and its contrast to the then prevailing Philo Vance school of detection. In a 1927 review of *The Benson Murder Case* Hammett expressed his opinion of S. S. Van Dine's gentleman detective: "There is a theory that any one who talks enough on any subject must, if only by chance, finally say something not altogether incorrect. Vance disproves this theory: he manages always, and usually ridiculously, to be wrong. His exposition of the technique employed by a gentleman shooting another gentleman who sits six feet in front of him deserves a place in a *How to be a detective by mail* course."

But there had been realists before—realism had been the dominant trend of American fiction for many decades—and there was little in Hammett's subject matter that was not familiar ground to half a dozen justly forgotten pulp writers. What was new about Hammett was his style, and it is his style that remains fresh. Consider the opening of "The Gatewood Caper," the first Continental Op story:

> Harvey Gatewood had issued orders that I was to be admitted as soon as I arrived, so it took me only a little less than fifteen minutes to thread my way past the doorkeepers, office boys,

Dell 129 (1946)
Artist: Gerald Gregg

> and secretaries who filled up most of the space between the Gatewood Lumber Corporation's front door and the president's private office. His office was large, all mahogany and bronze and green plush, with a mahogany desk as big as a bed in the center of the floor.

Allowing for changing styles of office furniture, this could as easily be the first paragraph of a Ross Macdonald novel. What distinguishes it from the work of Hammett's predecessors is the lightness of the writing, the way he starts in midstream, the use of colloquial language as the fundamental idiom rather than as something added for "color" or humor. Above all, there is the command of syntax that enables him to hit the essential details without getting bogged down in the needless ones. He gives a snapshot of the office—"all mahogany and bronze and green plush"—where a Dreiser might have given three pages of ponderous cataloging.

Beyond the efficiency of Hammett's prose, there is its beauty. His sensitivity to the physical qualities of language often endows his writing with the density of poetry—a cool, dry poetry he invented to express the neutrality of the world, the blankness of its materiality, and the way what happens in it seems to happen in a void:

> Green dice rolled across the green table, struck the rim together, and bounced back. One stopped short holding six white spots in two equal rows uppermost. The other tumbled out to the center of the table and came to rest with a single spot on top. . . .
>
> His way was uphill, up a hill frequently slippery, always uneven, through brush that tore his face and hands, caught his clothing. Three times he fell. He stumbled many times. The whistle did not come again. He did not find the Buick. He did not find the road along which he had come. (*The Glass Key*)
>
> Not much blood was in sight: a spot the size of a silver dollar around the hole the ice pick made in her blue silk dress. There was a bruise on her right cheek, just under the cheekbone. Another bruise, finger-made, was on her right wrist. Her hands

A NED BEAUMONT MYSTERY

211

pb

THE GLASS KEY

DASHIELL HAMMETT

Pocket Books 211 (1943)
Artist: Leo Manso

> were empty. I moved her enough to see that nothing was under her. . . .
>
> I kicked the pooch out of the way, made the opposite fence, untangled myself from a clothes line, crossed two more yards, got yelled at from a window, had a bottle thrown at me, and dropped into a cobblestoned back street. (*Red Harvest*)

With stripped-down syntax and a vocabulary reduced to basics, Hammett found original ways to convey a sense of physical and temporal immediacy. This prose mirrors the reality of duration, and consequently Hammett rarely dilates an instant of consciousness. His characters, caught up in the pace of the book, literally do not have time to think; they can only act.

By contrast, a Victorian writer like H. Rider Haggard, in all his forty-odd novels of physical adventure, was incapable of suggesting the feel of an action scene simply because his prose could not move fast enough. By unburdening himself of syntactical luggage, Hammett approximated actual tempo, as in this passage from *Red Harvest*: "Another car came around the limousine and charged us. Out of it, gunfire." Haggard would have needed at least half a page to say that, by which time (in Hammett's terms) the car would have been and gone.

Despite his eventual Marxist convictions (strong enough to lead him to a prison term he could have avoided, at an age when his health was already impaired), it would be difficult to speak of Hammett as a political writer. *Red Harvest* and *The Glass Key* describe American corruption in terms of a monstrous cynicism. Despite the presence of Wobblies and reform campaigns, there is nothing in either book that would give grounds for any kind of political faith. In Hammett's world, the morality of the hero is a doomed gesture (and with heroes like Ned Beaumont and Sam Spade and the Continental Op, that morality can itself be a rather dubious proposition).

Again and again, we are given the impression that events just happen, mindlessly and relentlessly, like the action of a huge and purposeless machine. It is a point of view like that of Flitcraft (in an oft-cited but unavoidable anecdote recounted in *The Maltese Falcon*), who nar-

Dell 486 (1951)
Artist: Robert Stanley

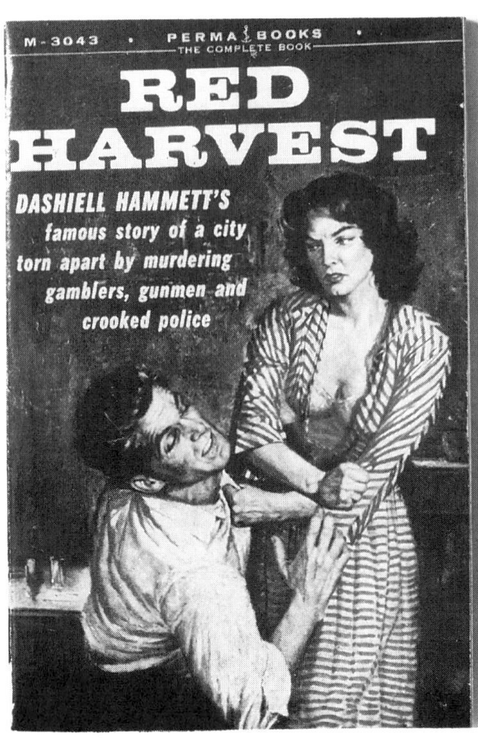

Perma M3043 (1956)
Artist: Lou Marchetti

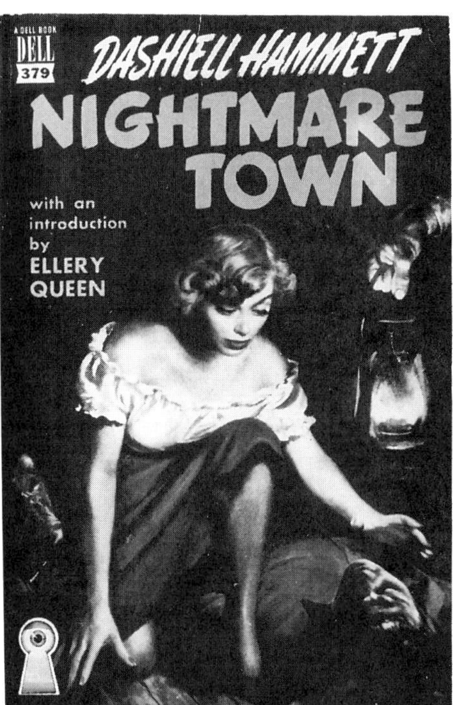

Dell 379 (1950)
Artist: Robert Stanley

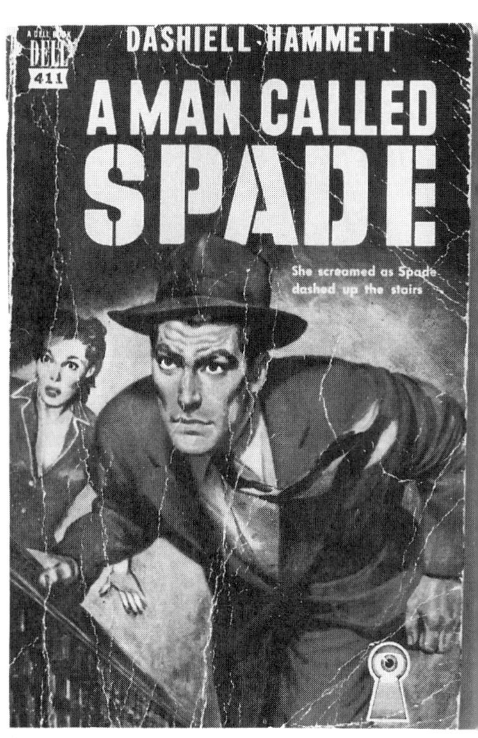

Dell 411 (1950)
Artist: Robert Stanley

rowly missed being crushed by a random falling beam: "He felt like somebody had taken the lid off life and let him look at the works." However deterministic his philosophy, Hammett was ultimately haunted by the sheer gratuitousness of life.

Hammett wrote his last book in 1933, six years before the advent of the paperbacks. But the height of his fame came in the 1940s, thanks to movies like *The Maltese Falcon*, the Sam Spade radio series (featuring the inimitable Howard Duff), and, not least, the wide dissemination of his novels and stories through Pocket Book and Dell editions. Though the covers changed to keep pace with the latest fashions, Hammett's words demonstrated their staying power against all the competition, a competition consisting largely of imitators of his work.

Among those imitators was not (as he took pains to clarify) James M. Cain, the other great tough-guy writer of the Depression era, who declared in his preface to *The Butterfly*: "I belong to no school, hard-boiled or otherwise, and I believe these so-called schools exist mainly in the imagination of critics, and have little correspondence in reality anywhere else. . . If he can write a book at all, a writer cannot do it by peeping over his shoulder at anybody else, any more than a woman can have a baby by watching some other woman have one. It is a genital process. . . I have read less than twenty pages of Mr. Dashiell Hammett in my whole life."

Cain was another chronicler of the gratuitousness of fate, in the sexual rather than the criminal sphere—but for Cain the two spheres are rarely far apart. In the typical Cain story, someone opens a door at random (and in the first paragraph) and his destiny is sealed then and there. Generally it is not long before he realizes what has happened, but, as if hypnotized, he does nothing to alter the course of events. Cain's best novels (*The Postman Always Rings Twice*, *Serenade*, *Double Indemnity*, *Career in C Major*) are in full gear from the first word and drive forward without a pause for breath until the final inevitable moment—the point where they click off neatly, leaving you with the void.

Pocket Books 443 (1947)

Avon 174 (1948)

> Here they come. Father McConnell says prayers help. If you've got this far, send up one for me, and Cora, and make it that we're together, wherever that is. (*The Postman Always Rings Twice*)

> They carried her out to a grave on the hillside. As they lowered her down, an iguana jumped out of it and went running over the rocks. (*Serenade*)

> I didn't hear the stateroom door open, but she's beside me now while I'm writing. I can feel her. The moon. (*Double Indemnity*)

In Cain's books, desire is all there is. His characters are sleepwalkers who flare into life as they experience a passionate impulse, and their life usually stops when the feeling stops. Small wonder that Cain is the author of *The Moth* and *The Butterfly*: he describes an insectlike existence without memory or intellect. When Frank Chambers in *Postman* wanders up to the roadside luncheonette, he is a man without a history and without an idea in his head. He is hungry and doesn't know where his next meal is coming from. He accepts a job from the owner of the luncheonette. The owner's wife walks in:

> Then I saw her. She had been out back, in the kitchen, but she came in to gather up my dishes. Except for the shape, she really wasn't any raving beauty, but she had a sulky look to her, and her lips stuck out in a way that made me want to mash them in for her.

Such is Cora, who is responsible for whatever else happens in the brief life of Frank Chambers. In typical fashion, she is described in terms not of physical appearance but of the effect she produces. According to Cain's notion, who cares what she actually looks like? The important thing is that Frank is prepared to kill for her. (Naturally, both the paperbacks and the movies ignored Cain's stipulation and made Cora into the one thing that could "explain" the mystery of her power—a raving beauty.)

Cain's heroes seem to rush toward their own destruction, but they themselves can never quite perceive it clearly. Frank Chambers, the down-and-out; Walter Huff, the insurance salesman (*Double Indemnity*); even John Howard Sharp, the opera singer (*Serenade*)—each in his way is thoroughly American—that is, straightforward, unreflective, and lecherous. Each is simply hooked:

> I looked into the fire a while then. I ought to quit, while the quitting was good, I knew that. But that thing was in me, pushing me still closer to the edge. (*Double Indemnity*)

If the Cain hero ultimately embraces his own catastrophe, it is because it is the most interesting thing that has ever happened to him.

The early novels are models of structure and concision: you cannot get much more laconic. *Postman* and *Double Indemnity* are relatively simple anecdotes, related by Cain at the exact length and tempo suitable to their nature, just enough so that the narrative breathes, without ever giving the reader time to get drowsy. In *Serenade* (1937), he tried

Avon 88 (1946)

Pocket Books 320 (1945)

something more daring, by compressing into 200 pages a narrative that a contemporary novelist would more likely expand to 800 or so (if not a five-volume epic with an accompanying miniseries). Only Cain could have managed with a straight face the successive transformations of the hero: from bum to pimp to great brutal lover to opera singer to movie star to tormented homosexual to fugitive from justice and ultimately to grief-stricken penitent. Cain responds to the operatic theme by creating a lyrical melodrama worthy of Puccini—which, although it has been mangled by the movies on several occasions, was never filmed as it should have been, as a hardboiled soap opera directed by Rainer Werner Fassbinder in his mode of Douglas Sirk imitation.

After his next book, the very funny *Career in C Major* (almost a farcical version of *Serenade*), Cain never quite recaptured the style he had created so expertly in his first five novels. There are moments here and there in *The Embezzler* and *Mildred Pierce*, but with each book the plots get increasingly ludicrous as the passion seems to sour. Later novels like *The Butterfly*, *Jealous Woman*, and *Galatea* are nearly unreadable.

In the absence of narrative control (not to mention the once bracing prose style), all that remains is the unpleasantness of the characters, so that one begins to understand Raymond Chandler's unjustifiably intemperate comment: "James Cain—faugh! Everything he touches smells like a billygoat. He is every kind of writer I detest, a faux naif, a Proust in greasy overalls, a dirty little boy with a piece of chalk and a board fence and nobody looking. Such people are the offal of literature, not because they write about dirty things, but because they do it in a dirty way."

Cain deserved better, of course, but Chandler's distaste is predictable. Raymond Chandler was a man whose character demanded a saving grace of nobility in the otherwise sordid world of the Philip Marlowe novels. For him, the detective hero "must be, to use a rather weathered phrase, a man of honor, by instinct, by inevitability, without thought of it, and certainly without saying it. He must be the best man in his world and a good enough man for any world . . . The story is his adventure in search of a hidden truth, and it would be no adventure if it did not happen to a man fit for adventure."

The tone of the passage from *The Simple Art of Murder* gives some idea of the intense (some would say self-deluded) moral seriousness of Chandler's approach to his craft, and of the unease he felt in the role of popular entertainer. In all his novels, one senses a desire to break through the conventions of the mystery genre, to transcend it somehow. Chandler's nature was constantly at war with his chosen form.

In any case, he lacked the fecundity of the typical pulp author, spending five months to write his first *Black Mask* story ("Blackmailers Don't Shoot"), recycling his earlier stories to create the plots of three of his novels, and writing with increasing difficulty as his career went on. Add to this the quiet miseries and barely articulated contradictions of his private life (set forth eloquently by Frank MacShane in *The Life of Raymond Chandler*) and you begin to get an idea of the odds against which he created the seven novels and the few dozen short stories that continue to keep his name alive.

The stories written during his pulp apprenticeship, for all their elegant rigor, look in retrospect like dry runs for what followed, laying out the elements of Chandler's world—decorative, geographic, verbal—without getting all the emotional juice from them. Even in the stories he "cannibalized" for his first three novels, where many of the details of plot and place and dialogue are the same, some central animating principle is missing, as if the invention of the name "Philip Marlowe" magically brought Chandler to the fullness of his powers. The protagonists of the earlier stories are intermittently similar to Marlowe, but they keep turning back into the usual tough pulp hero, wittier than most but equally vacuous. From the moment Marlowe makes his appearance, we are in the presence of a human being, no matter how idealized.

After all, when someone speaks of the Private Eye, it is generally Philip Marlowe he is talking about. Hammett's heroes—the Continental Op, Sam Spade, Ned Beaumont, Nick Charles—are the creatures of their particular narratives, having no imaginative life beyond them. Philip Marlowe, on the contrary, is the raison d'etre of Chandler's novels. The blondes and gunmen come and go; the dingy offices, the hallways, the dark parking lots and glittering nightclubs remain the same; bodies are discovered; guns poke out from behind curtains; Marlowe gets hit over the head; the plot develops as it always must; and it turns out to be the same story we have already heard. None of it would amount to much without the consciousness of Philip Marlowe. It is his presence as a living, thinking being that gives the books their life.

Chandler's concern with the sensitivity of his hero has been called sentimentality, but it is difficult to see where his books would be without it. Hammett, a natural yarn spinner, could send a poker-faced Continental Op through the bloody paces of *Red Harvest*, giving barely a hint of his character's reactions, save for one grim outburst: "I've got hard skin all over what's left of my soul, and after twenty years of messing around with crime I can look at any sort of a murder without seeing anything in it but my bread and butter, the day's work. But this getting a rear out of planning deaths is not natural to me. It's what this place has done to me."

The Hammett hero is completely externalized, and interior monologue has no place in his world. He has a code, but is no do-gooder; he is, at times, barely distinguishable from the criminals he deals with.

Marlowe, on the other hand, is unmistakably chivalrous, a quixotic figure who is also disillusioned and increasingly bitter. He is a man who perceives his own goodness as useless, and who is most himself when the heroism wears thin:

> I peeled off my coat and tie and sat down at the desk and got the office bottle out of the deep drawer and bought myself a drink. It didn't do any good. I had another, with the same result. . . .
>
> I began to feel a little less savage. I pushed things around on the desk. My hands felt thick and hot and awkward. I ran a finger across the corner of the desk and looked at the streak made by the wiping off of the dust. I looked at the dust on my finger and wiped that off. I looked at my watch. I looked at the wall. I looked at nothing.
>
> I put the liquor bottle away and went over to the washbowl to rinse the glass out. When I had done that I washed my hands and bathed my face in cold water and looked at it. The flush was gone from the left cheek, but it looked a little swollen. Not very much, but enough to make me tighten up again. I brushed my hair and looked at the gray in it. There was getting to be plenty of gray in it. The face under the hair had a sick look. I didn't like the face at all. (*The Lady in the Lake*)

What this oddly fragile hero is up against is a Los Angeles that Chandler knew well and hated ever more deeply, even as he extracted chunks of wondrously beautiful prose from its battered storefronts, chintzy nightclubs, and deserted hallways. He had grown up in England and cherished a notion of gentility that would probably have been out of place anywhere, but nowhere more so than in Los Angeles. The city gave Chandler something to focus his wit on—that angry and inventive wit which makes his letters such good reading and which flowers in some of the most bracing prose of the later novels:

> I ate dinner at a place near Thousand Oaks. Bad but quick. Feed 'em and throw 'em out. Lots of business. We can't bother with you sitting over your second cup of coffee, mister. You're using money space. See those people over there behind the rope? They want to eat. Anyway they think they have to. They

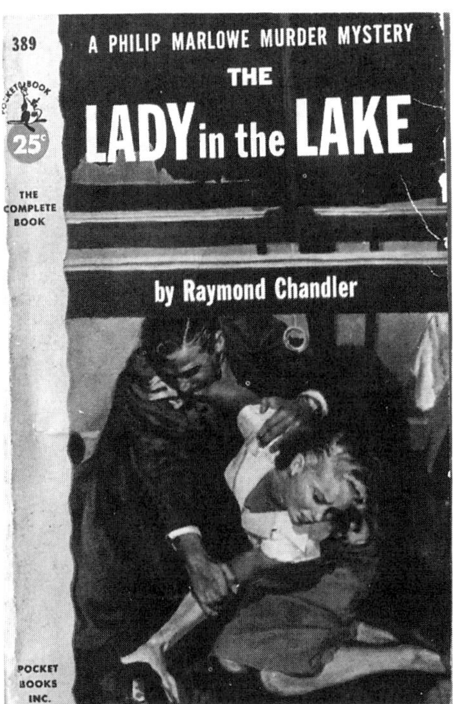

Pocket Books 389 (1954)
Artist: Tom Dunn

Pocket Books 916 (1952)
Artist: George Mayers

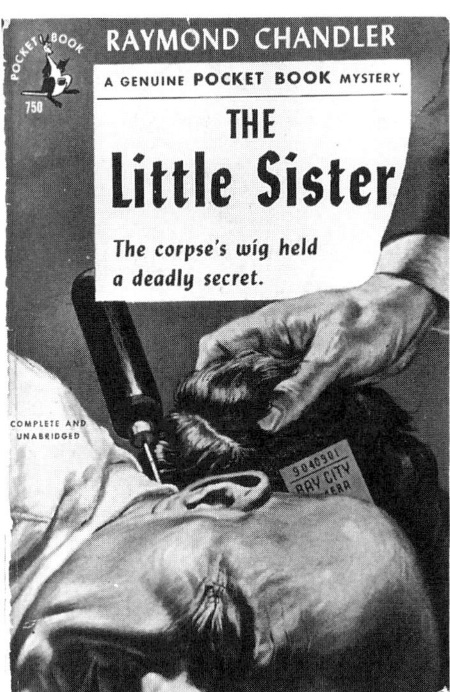

Pocket Books 750 (1951)
Artist: William Shoyer

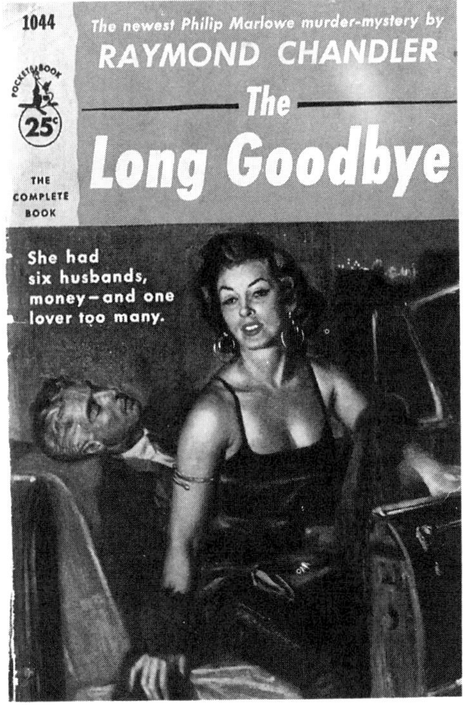

Pocket Books 1044 (1955)
Artist: Tom Dunn

> could do better home out of a can. They're just restless. Like you. They have to get the car out and go somewhere. Sucker-bait for the racketeers that have taken over the restaurants. Here we go again. You're not human tonight, Marlowe.
>
> I paid off and stopped in a bar to drop a brandy on top of the New York cut. Why New York, I thought. It was Detroit where they made machine tools. I stepped out into the night air that nobody had yet found out how to option. But a lot of people were probably trying. (*The Little Sister*)

The wit gives the books their energy, establishes their rhythm, which is comic. (Chandler often regretted that the element of self-parody in his works went unnoticed.) That comic energy in turn keeps it from becoming too apparent (for to do so would destroy the illusion on which the magic is founded) that what the Marlowe novels are finally about is simply loneliness in a sprawling city devoid of spiritual comforts. For a variety of reasons—greed, egotism, fear, selfish lust, or sheer thick-headedness—none of the people in the city can offer anything in the way of a human relationship. The gloom deepens in the last books, as the jokes get more bitter. At his death Chandler was trying to write a novel in which Marlowe fell in love and got married, a foredoomed attempt to somehow bring about a happy ending for a character who had always lacked any kind of companion.

In the extended arias of *The Little Sister* and *The Long Goodbye*, books in which Chandler made his great effort to get out of the trap he had made for himself—to bring the real world into his fiction—the detective hero collides with an ultimate sense of the void. The bright objects fade, the people turn brittle, a physically weakened Marlowe is left alone and without a future. For Chandler there could have been no other ending. It had already been foreshadowed in the eloquent passage that gives *The Big Sleep* its title:

> What did it matter where you lay once you were dead? In a dirty sump or in a marble tower on top of a high hill? You were dead, you were sleeping the big sleep, you were not bothered by things like that. Oil and water were the same as wind and air to you. You just slept the big sleep, not caring about

> the nastiness of how you died or where you fell. Me, I was part of the nastiness now . . .

As the hardboiled novel made its way into the movies and radio and television, it underwent a metamorphosis. The fast tempo, the wisecracking, the sexual innuendoes were played up, while the traces of gloom and revulsion were glossed over. The end product was a lighthearted entertainment like the TV series *77 Sunset Strip*.

The cardboard figure of the breezy shamus clowned and punched his way through a thousand paperback novels, a thousand scenarios, from Frank Gruber's Johnny Fletcher to Richard S. Prather's Shell Scott. The degree of witlessness in the wisecracking and of sadism in the punchouts varies from author to author, but the net effect is equally stultifying, no matter where you turn. Ninety-five percent of novelists get their ideas from the five percent who get their ideas from life, and the average fictional private eye is at least thrice removed from a fresh source of inspiration. A pall settles over the determined reader as he plows his way through the tired shenanigans of these animated clichés. Writing that tries to be lighthearted to order has a uniquely depressing effect. Often a very real ugliness begins to peep through—unredeemed because unperceived by the writer—and the would-be entertainment turns into something rather nasty and depleting.

Amid all the mechanical duplication of iconography, a few writers recorded their own visions. The work of those few remains readable to the extent that they made their own variations on the public myth, variations not often noticed in a market equally receptive to the well-worn. These writers make up a strange and melancholy collection of individuals—melancholy at least in part because of the sense of dissatisfaction with their own work that so often emerges. That dissatisfaction, shared by Hammett and Chandler, seems to haunt the hardboiled genre, in contrast to the verve and toughness of the foreground. The great American nightmare of Failure is never far off.

Consider, for example, the career of Horace McCoy, whose astonishing *They Shoot Horses, Don't They?* (1935) indicated the arrival of a rare kind of poet. McCoy revealed himself as the real nihilist of the hard-

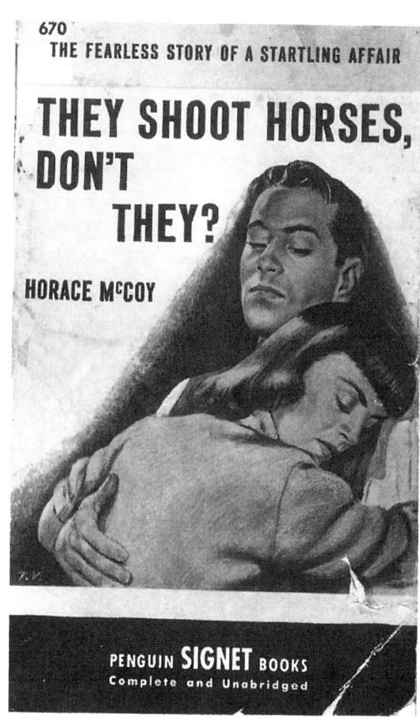

Signet 670 (1948)

Signet 884 (1951)
Artist: Ray Pease

boiled school, the laureate of the blank wall: "If you wanted to get rid of these things you had only to sit and stare at them with a fixed gaze . . . and they would begin receding."

When Signet published an abridged paperback edition of McCoy's *Kiss Tomorrow Goodbye* in 1949, the blurb declared: "Horace McCoy has been around. He's been a taxi driver, a war pilot, a wrestler, a body guard, a bouncer, a newspaperman, and a highly successful screen writer." But his characters do not share this richness of experience; they are marginal people whose ultimate desire is to surrender to blankness, to erase the world.

McCoy's strength, in his first and best book, lies in the precision with which he etches the world that is to be erased. *They Shoot Horses* operates on an almost exclusively physical level, as a meticulous rendering of a particular dance marathon in a particular Depression year, held on a particular pier jutting into a particular ocean. The soreness of the dancers' feet, the maddening repartee of the emcee, the fatigue and hysteria, and, above all, the monotony—that is the human world. Outside is the pier. There are two choices: to keep moving endlessly in circles or to step outside the circle and die. After 879 hours, the protagonists emerge from the dance hall:

> We walked around the side of the building onto the pier. It stretched out over the ocean as far as I could see, rising and falling and groaning and creaking with the movements of the water.
>
> "It's a wonder the waves don't wash this pier away," I said.
>
> "You're hipped on the subject of waves," Gloria said.
>
> "No, I'm not," I said.
>
> "That's all you've been talking about for a month—"
>
> "All right, stand still a minute and you'll see what I mean. You can feel it rising and falling—"
>
> "I can feel it without standing still," she said, "but that's no reason to get yourself in a sweat. It's been going on for a million years."
>
> "Don't think I'm crazy about this ocean," I said. "It'll be all right with me if I never see it again. I've had enough ocean to last me the rest of my life."

Death, like Gloria's voluntary death a few paragraphs later, means nothing, but comes as a relief, since no one can see much point in being alive. Small wonder that in France McCoy was classed with Hemingway and Faulkner. The postwar *philosophes* were inclined to see what no American critic of the time would have noticed—that McCoy had penetrated deeper than anyone into the zero state at the heart of the hardboiled novel. He had produced a sharp, dry, arbitrary kind of book, a book poised so precisely on the edge of the real that it seems to cancel itself out.

The point of view in his later books remains equally bleak. They have at their heart a feeling of profound lassitude; impulses of violence and resistance to the world spin in a rut and wear themselves out to nothing. Yet it cannot be said that any of these later novels—*No Pockets in a Shroud* (1937), *I Should Have Stayed Home* (1938), and *Kiss Tomorrow Goodbye* (1948)—succeeds on anything like the level of the first. Sporadically they attain the same sharpness, but just as sporadi-

Signet 754 (1949)
Artist: James Avati

cally the protagonists drift in and out of character, and the situations rearrange themselves with a casualness that verges on the improvisatory. *Kiss Tomorrow Goodbye*, McCoy's most obviously ambitious novel, foreshadows Jim Thompson in its portrait of a brilliant college-educated psychopath busily weaving his own elaborate doom, and its scenes of graft and blackmail have a nice cold edge before McCoy's prose sinks with almost suicidal inevitability into that Freudian/Faulknerian morass which was a pitfall for many Forties novelists. His other writing consists of *Scalpel* (a more or less unreadable attempt to cash in on the then current *Not As a Stranger*/Frank Slaughter medical cycle) and the posthumously published *Corruption City*, which is merely an undistinguished treatment from McCoy's Paramount days (it was filmed by William Dieterle as *The Turning Point* in 1952) packaged as a novel. (One of the few high points of McCoy's long movie career was the script he cowrote for Nicholas Ray's *The Lusty Men*, a gloomy meditation on rodeo life made in 1952.)

It is not, finally, as much of an achievement as his talent warranted. But it remained evident almost to the end that he cared a great deal about prose. He had a knack of describing objects, buildings, landscapes with a casual exactness that seems to make them vanish. At such moments he arrives at an intuitive approximation of the Buddhist doctrine of the voidness of phenomena, a doctrine peculiarly apposite to the novel of action.

Kenneth Fearing was another who brought his own quirks to a usually standardized form. For a poet of Fearing's propensities—politically radical but resolutely undoctrinaire, and attracted by a brand of nightmare comedy in which the trivia of America suddenly loom grotesquely enlarged—the thriller was a convenient medium. It enabled him to dwell on precisely those details of ordinary life that fascinated him, and to place them in the appropriate context of death and crime. The poet Kenneth Rexroth wrote of him: "Kenneth Fearing didn't think like an advertising copywriter. He thought like the advertising copy itself, or at least like a taxi driver reading a billboard while fighting traffic." The descriptive intensity of some of Fearing's poetry does not differ greatly from the style of his mysteries:

Bantam 738 (1949)

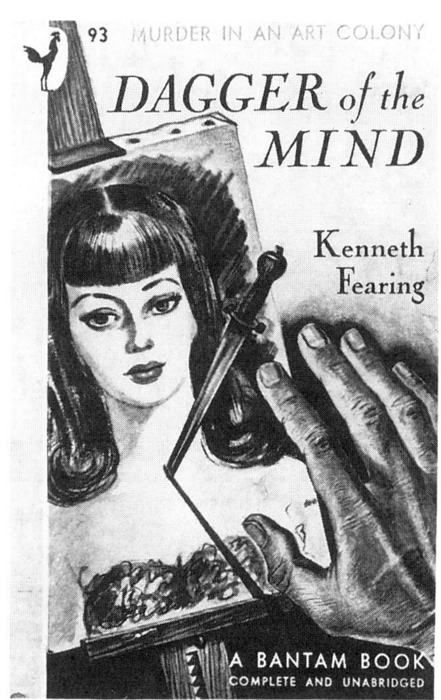

Bantam 93 (1946)
Artist: Paul Galdone

And here we are, four lost and forgotten customers in this time
that surely will never again be found,
Sitting, at ten-foot intervals, along this lost and forgotten bar
(Wishing the space were further still, for we are still too close
for comfort),
Knowing that the bartender, and the elk's head, and the picture
of some forgotten champion
(All gazing at something of interest beyond us and behind us,
but very far away),
Must somehow be aware of us, too, as we stare the cold interior of our lives reflected in the mirror beneath and in back
of them—

("4 a.m.," *Stranger at Coney Island*, 1948)

Indeed, in some of his poetry the language of hardboiled fiction is carried over unchanged, as in the brilliant "How Do I Feel?" from the 1938 collection *Dead Reckoning*, which begins:

Get this straight, Joe, and don't get me wrong.

Sure, Steve, O.K., all I got to say is, when do I get the dough?

Will you listen for a minute? And just shut up? Let a guy explain?

Go ahead, Steve, I won't say a word.

In *The Big Clock* (1946), Fearing evoked the world of glossy magazine editors and copywriters, and showed them to be as much creatures of delusion as the abstracted "masses" they pandered to. Fearing had worked briefly for *Time* and here retaliated by detailing the manic bureaucracy of Janoth Enterprises, headed by the more than slightly megalomaniac Earl Janoth (a murderous stand-in for Henry Luce):

> What we decided in this room, more than a million of our fellow citizens would read three months from now, and what they read they would accept as final. They might not know they were doing so, they might even briefly dispute our decisions, but still they would follow the reasoning we presented, remember phrases, the tone of authority, and in the end their crystallized judgements would be ours.
>
> Where our own logic came from, of course, was still another matter. The moving impulse simply arrived, and we, on the face that the giant clock turned to the public, merely registered the correct hour of the standard time.
>
> But being the measure by which so many lives were shaped and guided gave us, sometimes, strange delusions.

Though he was in a way a dilettante of the crime novel, Fearing proved himself a capable storyteller in *The Big Clock*—at least until the last few pages, when he appears to have surrendered to an attack of massive indifference and let the plot pretty much take care of itself. The story's chief mechanism—the hunter forced to hunt himself—has certainly proved serviceable to many others since, notably Orson Welles in *Mister Arkadin*: not that the device was new with Fearing, having already been given an ingenious workout only a year earlier in Samuel Fuller's novel *The Dark Page* (later filmed by Phil Karlson as *Scandal Sheet*). That particular device also lent itself beautifully to Fearing's vision of white-collar backbiting and paranoia (seasoned with acute sexual unease), a vision which has lost none of its accuracy. Fearing's own point of view is never in doubt:

> *Newsways*, *Commerce*, *Crimeways*, *Personalities*, *The Sexes*, *Fashions*, *Futureways*, the whole organization was full and overrunning with frustrated ex-artists, scientists, farmers, writers, explorers, poets, lawyers, doctors, musicians, all of whom spent their lives conforming, instead. And conforming to what? To a sort of overgrown, aimless, haphazard stenciling apparatus that kept them running to psychoanalysts, sent them to insane asylums, gave them high blood pressure, stomach ulcers, killed them off with cerebal hemorrhages and heart failure, sometimes suicide. Why should I pay still more tribute to this fatal machine? It would be easier and simpler to get squashed stripping its gears than to be crushed helping it along.

If *The Big Clock* was Fearing's revenge on the conformists and organization men, *Dagger of the Mind* (1941), which Raymond Chandler called "a savage piece of intellectual double-talk," allowed him his licks at an assortment of would-be artists and thinkers congregated at an art colony established by a wealthy patron (Fearing, it should be noted, was a frequent guest at the Yaddo colony in Saratoga). It is also a highly amusing parody of the corpse-at-the-garden-party school of suspense, with an esteemed literary critic as the victim of choice. Fearing makes the most of his opportunities, particularly when he has to deal with his protagonist, Christopher Bartel, the ultimate hard-drinking hero:

> I poured a stiff drink for myself. There are times, I've noticed, when a fellow has to be sober and think like lightning, and if you happen to be drunk, or a little drunk, the only thing to do is to take three or four more shots and, well, to put it simply, drink yourself sober.

The progress of Christopher's drinking becomes a counterpoint to the progress of the plot, vital elements of which begin to disappear from his memory:

> I tried to figure out whether I was ahead or behind in my usual drinking schedule. My arms felt like a pair of feather dusters and my head felt like the Hayden Planetarium. The feeling was good, and I decided I was behind the schedule, merely tapering off, as I'd decided I ought to do.

And when Christopher (for reasons too complex to be described here) finds himself condemned to death, these (as he prepares for his demise with a contraband bottle of Scotch) are his last reflections:

> With a couple more drinks, I felt, I'd have the solution . . . There was a plate of grouse and a quart of Scotch. While it lasted, I was a man with a future. And by the time it was gone I'd have the answer to this present jam, an answer that would be perfectly simple . . . And then after I'd decided that, I had another drink, and realized I'd been kidding myself. All the way along, not only today, but during the last months, and in fact, all of my life. The minute a person is born, any person, he is in the middle of a jam, and there is no way out of it except through death.

Such is Fearing's archetypal individual in the universe, and such the joke buried under all his other jokes.

Jonathan Latimer was a more straightforward kind of joker, whose roughhouse blend of murder and farce made him a great favorite in the Thirties, before he switched from novels to screenplays. Latimer was an odd and original writer, who could (in *Sinners and Shrouds*) get lyrical about a men's room ("Gray light, filtered through glazed windows, gave urinals and washbasins a ghostly appearance as though they were illuminated by some inner radiance of their own"). His trademark, in books like *The Lady in The Morgue*, was a deadpan black humor of his own devising ("The reporter from the *City Press* was named Jerry

Johnson. His face had an unhealthy pallor; his black eyes were set deep in discolored sockets; he was drinking himself to death as fast as he could on a salary of twenty-six dollars a week.").

Alcoholism and sex and the generic absurdities of mystery plotting were Latimer's running jokes. On the Pocket Books edition of *The Lady in the Morgue*, a blurb identifies the hero as "Detective Crane—Unique and Alcoholic." There are still some good laughs in the Crane novels—*Murder in the Madhouse*, *Headed for a Hearse*, *The Lady in the Morgue*, and *The Dead Don't Care*—even if the bloom has faded considerably, and if too many of the gags take the easiest stereotypical targets, from brainless blondes to incompetent Filipino houseboys. Still, at their best the books have the tempo of a 1932 Warner Brothers movie; you can almost hear Lee Tracy or Roscoe Karns spitting out the dialogue.

Latimer shifted gears a bit with *Solomon's Vineyard* (published in somewhat bowdlerized form in 1941 as *The Fifth Grave*), a rougher and kinkier version of Hammett's *The Dain Curse*, populated by a group of California cultists who prefigure the Charles Manson era, and featuring (in the uncensored version) some unrestrained sadomasochistic love-making. Thereafter Latimer devoted himself to writing for the movies; his screenplays included excellent adaptations of Hammett's *The Glass Key* (1942) and Fearing's *The Big Clock* (1947), as well as the serpentine 1947 thriller *They Won't Believe Me*. He broke his silence as a novelist with *Sinners and Shrouds* (1955) and *Black Is the Fashion for Dying* (1959), blandly entertaining though far from original mysteries. They confirm him as a thorough professional and can still surprise now and again with patches of verbal beauty (like this from *Sinners and Shrouds*) in a style Latimer had never fully explored:

> Excited voices soared from near-by houses. A bulb, turned on back of a second-story window, lit the mist overhead. A door slammed somewhere. In the cottage, shrill above music, the telephone began to ring. Clay backed into the mist, turned and started for the street. A rose bush tugged at his coat, scratched his hand; crushed tulips made sighing noises under his feet. He began to run as he neared the sidewalk.

Latimer could make music with that distinctive "thing-language" of the hardboiled novel, and it is regrettable that he took no more than occasional stabs at it.

If the makers of B movies waited a long time to get their due, the writers of B novels had to endure an even longer penance. Consider the case of David Goodis. At a time when all over the world (at least the part of it that has money and energy to devote to the Film As Art), retrospectives and scholarly articles were exploring the movies adapted from Goodis novels—by François Truffaut (*Shoot the Piano Player*), Delmer Daves (*Dark Passage*), Jacques Tourneur (*Nightfall*), and Paul Wendkos (*The Burglar*)—the novels themselves remained inaccessible. Only long after Goodis's death in obscurity was a portion of his work once again made available to American readers, and its continued availability is by no means a sure thing.

Not that I would call Goodis an unflawed writer. There was undoubtedly more promise at the outset of his career than accomplishment at the end, and he seems indeed to have followed the downward course charted by so many of his characters. The Kafkaesque first para-

Dell 221 (1948)

Gold Medal 652(1957)
Artist: Barye Phillips

Gold Medal 348 (1953)

Gold Medal 623 (1956)
Artist: Mitchell Hooks

Lion 124 (1953)

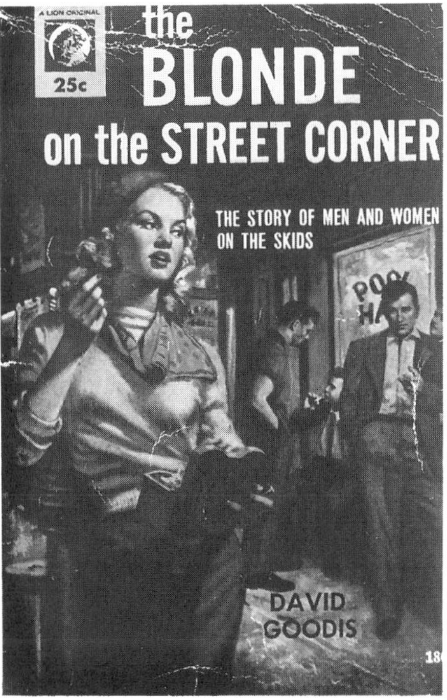

Lion 186 (1954)

graph of *Dark Passage* (1946) already established his characteristic air of ineluctable doom:

> It was a tough break. Parry was innocent. On top of that he was a decent sort of guy who never bothered people and wanted to lead a quiet life. But there was too much on the other side and on his side of it there was practically nothing. The jury decided he was guilty. The judge handed him a life sentence and he was taken to San Quentin.

"On top of that he was a decent sort of guy who never bothered people and wanted to lead a quiet life"—the same could be said of all Goodis' heroes. But, bad-luck champions that they are, their extraordinary efforts to stay out of trouble lead them straight into it. If they survive the first blow and find a refuge where their wounds can heal, a second blow is sure to be waiting.

Goodis was one of the most distinctive writers of paperback originals. A single page of his work is instantly recognizable, as much for its prose style as for its recurring obsessions. He wrote of winos and barroom piano players and small-time thieves in a vein of tortured lyricism all his own, whose very excesses seemed uniquely appropriate to the subject matter. As his titles announce—*Street of the Lost*, *Street of No Return*, *The Wounded and the Slain*, *Down There*—he was a poet of the losers, transforming swift cut-rate melodramas into traumatic visions of failed lives. The desperation of his characters appears to have been that of their creator:

> Aside from the pay, it was emotionally important for Cassidy to do this type of work. Keeping his eyes on the road and his mind on the wheel was a protective fence holding him back from internal as well as external catastrophe.

Isn't this Goodis speaking directly, not about driving a bus, but about his own writing? It is precisely that sense of impending internal catastrophe that distinguishes his books. We read them above all for the steady and undeniable emotional drive that at times handles language with something like hysteria, or that subsides into distinctive plangent largoes.

Goodis had no great gift for physical description, and was no good at describing how something works. His plots were devoid of ingenuity. His characters were always the same few, repeated obsessionally from book to book. But he did convey that anguish, the anguish of his characters' distance from reality. His hero is a frightened, lonely, unworldly, often alcoholic man. He smokes cigarette after cigarette. He walks the streets and never meets a friend. He sits alone in a hotel room staring out the window, or he throws himself into meaningless work and tries to shut out the rest of the world:

> Plyne looked, seeing the thirty-a-week musician who sat there at the battered piano, the soft-eyed, soft-mouthed nobody whose ambitions and goals aimed at exactly zero, who'd been working here three years without asking or even hinting for a raise. . . . It was almost as though he wasn't there and the piano was playing all by itself. Regardless of the action at the tables or the bar, the piano man was out of it, not even an observer. . . . Even the smile was something neutral. It was never aimed at a woman. It was aimed very far out there beyond all tangible targets, really far out there beyond the leftfield bleachers. (*Down There*)

His own life, long hidden, has become a little clearer thanks to the researches of Philippe Garnier, whose biography of Goodis (*Goodis: La Vie en Noir et Blanc*, as yet untranslated into English) dredges up the secret corners of a life very much out of the public eye. As far as the world at large was concerned, Goodis pretty much fell through the cracks, and on the basis of Garnier's account one's impression is that he wanted it that way. His career was not so much the *Retreat from Oblivion* that his first novel proclaimed as it was a voluntary and secretive descent into oblivion.

Clearly he was not without ambition. At first he aimed for acceptance as a serious novelist, and did at least achieve a measure of success with *Dark Passage*, which led to a three-year stint as a Warner Brothers scriptwriter. It was in this early period that he produced perhaps his most nearly perfect book, the spare, balanced, and inexplicably moving *Nightfall* (1947). The plot line—another innocent man on the run, as in *Dark Passage*—could not be more routine. But in *Nightfall* Goodis creates an atmosphere where everything is symbolic—the oppressive heat of a summer night, a metal box of watercolors that crashes to the floor, the winding staircase where words of betrayal are overheard, the mountains toward which the hero flees—and at the same densely literal.

By the time he left Warners in 1950 (it isn't clear whether he quit or was let go) his career—indeed, his whole life—was evidently going into reverse gear. He settled into ten years of paperback originals, mostly for Gold Medal books. There is no evidence that he had high artistic goals in mind. More likely he chose a kind of fiction which would support him while guaranteeing a cloak of anonymity. With the move to paperback originals, the style and contents of his books changed radically. As if mirroring the failure of Goodis's higher literary ambitions, the novels turned decisively toward the lower depths. From here on he would be the chronicler of skid row, and specifically of the man fallen from his social class: the disgraced airline pilot (*Cassidy's Girl*), the artist turned art appraiser for a gang of burglars (*Black Friday*), the famous crooner turned streetcorner bum (*Street of No Return*), the concert performer turned barroom piano player (*Down There*). In this fashion David Goodis, great literary artist turned streetcorner hack writer, could tell his own story and ply his trade at the same time.

Cassidy's Girl (1951), the first and apparently the most popular of his paperbacks, contains most of the elements of the subsequent novels: an environment of grinding poverty, a sensitive but inarticulate male protagonist largely unaware of his self-destructive tendencies, and two women who divide his energies, with melodramatic consequences: one of them a frail ghostly alcholic haunted by unrealizable dreams (let us call her Type A), the other (Type B) a fat, rough-tongued, hard-drinking (and hard-fighting) woman who will stop at nothing to keep the hero to herself. There are many recurring relationships in Goodis's novels, but this polarity between two images of woman is always central; and the hero, caught up by his own lack of self-knowledge, is usually destroyed by it. He sees Type A as his true love, his only hope for happiness, from whom he is kept apart by Type B, who holds him in bondage through marriage, blackmail, or even the threat of physical force. What he can never admit is that he himself in some way sets up the no-win situation, and that indeed it is the Type B woman, that obese and muscular caricature of female dominance, that he really desires.

The novels which followed were by no means all on the same level. *The Burglar* (1953) stands out for its evocation of a Romantic death-wish in the context of a disposable drama of low-grade crooks coming unraveled in the wake of a bungled break-in, an evocation which culminates memorably in an offshore *Liebestod* in Atlantic City. *The Burglar*'s prose style is notable as well: Goodis seems really to have worked on this one, piling on little flourishes of syncopation that remind us how musical his ear could be. If Jack Kerouac had written crime novels they might have sounded a bit like this, as bop prosody modulates the stark lines of pulp narration. *Black Friday*—a more elaborate variation on *The Burglar*—shows Goodis at a similar peak of tonal control. Here his sense of the criminal band as a world apart, with its own hermetic codes of respect and kinship, informs every action in the book. Outside the law there is no freedom, only a stifling web of compulsions and obligations.

It was in the 1954 Gold Medal original *Street of No Return* that Goodis came closest to acknowledging that his heroes' tragic destinies were largely self-created. By Goodis's standards, *Street of No Return* (which Samuel Fuller turned into a flamboyant film too rarely seen) ranks almost as an epic, a wino's odyssey from nowhere to nowhere. Three bums stand on a corner trying to figure out how to get a drink. One of them, Whitey, wanders off and comes back 175 pages later, a bottle under his coat, having relived his entire life: his career as a pop singer shattered by an obsessive love for a prostitute, his torture by racketeers and his beating at the hands of the police, his final turn as reluctant hero foiling a conspiracy to foment a race riot—only to find that all he really wants to do is go back to the corner. The battered Whitey finally admits to himself: "You've played a losing game and actually enjoyed the idea of losing, almost like them freaks who get their kicks when they're banged around . . . You're in that same bracket, buddy. You're one of them less-than-nothings who like the taste of being hurt."

In his final works—*Fire in the Flesh*, *Night Squad*, *Somebody's Done For*—Goodis shows every sign of having reached a personal impasse. The obsessions laid bare in his novels begin to repeat themselves rather than developing creatively. But taken as a whole his writing represents an astonishing example of self-revelation in the context of commercial fiction. Anyone who spends some time with his books learns to identify their peculiarly intense atmosphere, their outbursts of eloquence, their sense of the world as an abyss made for falling into. His best books have a unique poetry of solitude and fear. They read like the improvisations of someone compelled to keep writing, to keep the words, the pages coming toward him. He writes knowing that he must fill the page, finish the episode, continue as far as the next episode, the next book. His central image is ultimately that of the wounded man, his strength gone, pulling himself forward, yet sensing that he won't make it, that it will all have been in vain. That such testaments of deprivation and anxiety could have sustained a career as a paperback novelist is today cause for wonderment. Nothing so downbeat, so wedded to reiterations of personal and social failure, would be likely to find a mass market publisher at present. The absolutely personal voice of David Goodis seems to have escaped almost by accident, emanating startlingly from the heart of an efficient entertainment industry, like the wailing of an outcast.

In mystery and hardboiled fiction, the transition from the Thirties to the Forties is unmistakable. Cain and Hammett and McCoy deal in a clear unblinking light. Objects are delineated against the quietly terrifying neutrality of a noon sky, and actions equally neutral—be they a suicide or a walk across a verandah. They deal as well in speed, in deadpan wisecracks that add another kind of brightness.

Then, with the 1940s, comes the Great Fear. The light is shadowed over; for ten years the key words will be "night" and "dark." The hardboiled wry grimace will be replaced by abject terror, by a sense of ultimate impotence in a world suddenly full of danger, of nothing but danger. In Hammett's novels there are conspiracies, but there is nothing mysterious about them. They are part of the everyday violence of an everyday corrupt city, and they need no superhuman powers, secret weapons, or network of invisible agents to make themselves felt. In Raymond Chandler's books, the menace is vaguer, more all-embracing, more redolent of primitive terror—the world is a vast spider's web. A postwar writer like David Goodis writes of fear as if it were the only emotion his heroes were capable of experiencing.

It is in this context that we should approach the work of Dorothy B. Hughes, which in the 1940s enjoyed a critical reputation somewhat bewildering today. Hughes started out as a poet. (She was in fact the Yale Younger Poet of 1931, her winning volume appropriately titled *Dark Certainty*.) A decade later, in 1940, she published her first mystery, *The So Blue Marble*, and was from the start successful both as a novelist and as an inexhaustible source of movie material.

Her narratives lack the logical coherence that would today be demanded of a children's cartoon. She revels in pulpish scientific inventions that can do whatever the plot demands of them, and in shadowy networks of criminals or spies that are almost literally omnipresent. Double identities are so commonplace in her work that one ceases to notice them after a while. In general her plotting is so loose and evidently improvisatory that it loses the very name of plotting. Once it becomes clear that anything at all can happen, the outcome is no longer a matter of great anxiety.

And yet—and despite literary mannerisms that compound the flaws of construction—there is something at large in Hughes's books, something as insubstantial as a mood, which does indeed grip. It is a remote echo of the terror of that time, and, if her plotting has become unreal to us, perhaps that terror has become unreal as well—for the moment.

In her books the terror often begins somewhere in New York. A fair number of crime writers have used New York as a setting, but none is really identified with it. L.A. had Chandler (and shares Ross Macdonald with a string of southern Californian suburbs); San Francisco had Hammett, Chicago Jonathan Latimer, Philadelphia David Goodis. Boston has come up with Robert Parker's Spenser, and John D. MacDonald took care of business for the whole state of Florida (at least until Elmore Leonard, Charles Willeford, James W. Hall, and Carl Hiaasen came along). But the Manhattan that was home to Mickey Spillane's Mike Hammer was too distorted to qualify as a real place, while Ed McBain chose to cloak the quite convincing locale of his 87th Precinct series under the pseudonym of Isola. Dorothy B. Hughes' contribution was to impart a certain dreamy clarity to the geography of midtown

Pocket Books 587 (1949)
Artist: Frank McCarthy

Manhattan, where (in *The Delicate Ape*) "The man came out of the front doors of the great and gray Pennsylvania Station into the early night." And in a moment, as always, he will hear footsteps a few yards behind him and will know that They are right behind him.

In *The So Blue Marble*, They are otherworldly characters of indeterminate nationality who want to lay their hands on the tiny blue marble that contains "hieroglyphs telling the secrets of the greatest lost civilization, of the day when the sun was harnessed, as we would like to harness it, when gravitation was controlled as we haven't dreamed of controlling it." In *The Fallen Sparrow*, They are Spanish Fascists on the trail of a Loyalist veteran who knows where ancient riches are buried. They will stop at nothing; They are urbane and on intimate terms with the Park Avenue aristocracy; They are ubiquitous and all-powerful. Somehow, in the end, They lose (usually by the kind of sleight-of-hand favored by the Amazing Spider-Man).

But lyricism they had, these novels, with their rain and shadow and Park Avenue and Madison Avenue suddenly places of fear, and with their sudden eruptions of dream material into an orderly salon (the poet's legacy). Maybe no one will ever be frightened by her books again, but they will perhaps be reminded of a surrounding world—the one she wrote in—far more frightening than her own childlike, sometimes magical, adventures.

Cornell Woolrich (who also wrote under the names William Irish and George Hopley) is another of the writers whom the French have helped salvage from oblivion, and whom Truffaut filmed with varying success in *The Bride Wore Black* and *Mississippi Mermaid* (adapted from *Waltz Into Darkness*). Woolrich has in fact been a primary source for the movies: *Rear Window*, *Phantom Lady*, *The Night Has a Thousand Eyes*, *Street of Chance* (from *The Black Curtain*), *Fear in the Night* (from the story "Nightmare"), *No Man of Her Own* (from *I Married a Dead Man*), *The Black Angel*, and countless other films have been based on his novels and stories. Truth to tell, the films are often more effective than the originals, because, although Woolrich had a genius for inventing extraordinary situations (Raymond Chandler called him "the best idea

Gold Medal 136 (1951)
Artist: Barye Phillips

man"), he wrote too often in a bloated purple prose that thuds like overemphatic movie music:

> Death has begun. Darkness has begun, there in the full jonquil-blaze of the dinner-table candles. Darkness. A spot no bigger at first than that spilled drop of consomme. Growing, steadily growing, by the days, by the weeks, by the months, until it has blotted out everything else. Until all is darkness. Until there is nothing *but* darkness. Darkness and fear and pain, doom and death. (*Night Has a Thousand Eyes*)

It might be tolerable in small doses, but Woolrich writes this way the whole time. Yet through all the crudities of style and excesses of melodrama, something in his work fascinates. He is quite simply the premier paranoid among crime writers. His is the realm of the impossible coincidence, perceived as a cosmic joke at the expense of man. Even if he writes of thugs and dives and dark city streets, he is miles away from any kind of naturalism; in his world there are magical correspondences between things rather than logical relations.

The perennial unanswered question of his protagonists is: Why me? Why should my husband of five minutes be shot dead on the church steps? Why should my angelic bride turn out to be a vicious murderer? The hero of *Phantom Lady* quarrels with his wife, steps out to a neighborhood bar, and strikes up a conversation with a beautiful woman. He returns home to find his wife dead and himself accused of her murder. When he offers his bar encounter as an alibi, the woman cannot be found, and the people who were in the bar at the time—a demonstrably random assortment of human beings—all deny having seen her.

This comes close to being the classic Woolrich situation. Although the solution is inevitably disappointing (the witnesses have been bribed to keep silent by the real murderer), there remains one further revealing stroke of plotting: the phantom lady is not found, and does not step forward to clear the hero, because she is actually a hopeless lunatic who on that one evening, in a rare spell of lucidity, had wandered out by herself. This is another of the million-to-one chances that are the essence of Woolrich's stories, like the train wreck that kills a happily married couple in *I Married a Dead Man* or the arbitrary bits of evidence that combine to falsely convince the returning soldier of his wife's infidelity in the cruel story, "The Light in the Window."

For Woolrich, these disasters are meaningless pranks of the gods, and it is always the innocent who are singled out as victims. His work offers testimony of a life lived in fear, a life such as many lead but few have described. He himself (as described in a style of almost Woolrichian excess by Michael Avallone) "lived some forty years of his time in a hotel room; he had no close personal friends and the Big Romance always eluded him; some of his most memorable works are dedicated to such lifeless things as hotel rooms, typewriters, and the utter sadness of the human condition; later on in life he discovered John Barleycorn and the empty days and nights of his withdrawal from society echoed and re-echoed with the typical alcoholic *miseria* of broken appointments, paranoiac harangues and self-lashing which ended in the usual weeping haze of '*Where did I go wrong?*'"

His hero is such a man as himself, whose exactness of perception serves only to intensify an overwhelming sense of impotence and doom. It is strange to think that this prolific and highly successful author of popular thrillers was really offering his readers nothing but despair and the longing for extinction. It cannot be said that he exploited paranoia as a literary device; it was in all sincerity his way of perceiving the world.

Woolrich is an extreme case, but an interesting one because his paranoia accorded so well with the mood of the time. His best books were written between 1940 and 1948, and this was the period in which, concurrent with the Second World War and its aftermath, a great change came over the American consciousness. In many of its aspects, it can be perceived as a morbid gloom which even prosperity and political hegemony could not dispel. This change was to be reflected in phenomena as diverse as the postwar film noir and the overt paranoia which attached itself to the anti-Communist crusade, and not least in the changing tone of paperback novels.

Chapter Five

The Paperback Detective and His Discontent

Carl Jung described a state in which the mind, through fatigue or confusion, lays itself open to "the overpowering of consciousness by the autonomous contents of the unconscious." This is the state in which the line between reality and fantasy blurs, and the images within gain ascendancy and are perceived as real. Something like this *abaissement du niveau mental* appears to have happened on a national scale in postwar America.

Its progression can be traced in the popular culture. The Thirties pulp imagery of secret societies bent on world domination, mad sadistic scientists, and bloody avengers is plainly fantastic, but by the late Forties these images are taken as utterly real, just as the rocket ships of *Flash Gordon* and *Buck Rogers* become actual cigar-shaped phenomena seen in the sky.

The invasion of the German consciousness by demonic imagery, and the fruits of that invasion, were things that Americans were in no way prepared to understand. The hells of Auschwitz and Hiroshima intruded strangely on the childlike universe of Major Bowes and Kay Kyser. Reality rushed in on the world of fantasy; and, the barrier between them broken, the two flowed together. Since the unbelievable had already happened, henceforth anything could be believed.

The Thirties pulp hero in mask and cape, battling the Purple Menace or the Green Menace, has by 1947 become a down-to-earth Mike Hammer battling the Red Menace. Fantasy has become reality. At a single psychic stroke the tawdry street is transformed into a mythological arena. Gone are Shangri-La, Oz, Disney's Magic Forest. Even attempts (in Hollywood) to revive Arabian Nights fantasies fall apart and dissolve into their elements of wiseguy comedy and softcore pornography. Gone are the visionary landscapes and sensuous charms of a film such as Alexander Korda's *The Thief of Bagdad*. For the moment, the ugliness of the world has triumphed over all attempts to hide from it.

The ultrareal, the undeniable sordid surfaces of everyday places and everyday lives, suddenly glow strangely and at once are numinous. It is as if everybody were hungry for reality, although this has nothing to do with realism; it has, however, everything to do with the new palpable fleshiness of every popular art form, like the three-dimensional fists and torsos that protrude from the book covers. It is a kind of fever, and the afflicted look for something very solid indeed, as if materiality in itself would cure them or stabilize them. Theology having failed, it becomes witchcraft's turn.

In such an atmosphere, the pulp imagination can rise to new heights of glory. An L. Ron Hubbard can move from second-rate science fiction to the founding of a would-be worldwide religion. A hack thriller writer like Howard Hunt can end up acting out his fantasies as national policy at the Bay of Pigs and the Watergate. And in Mickey Spillane, the most successful author of his day, the hardboiled novel comes full circle: a genre that originated in a concern for realism now provides the trappings for the wildest of fantasizing.

Spillane is notable for having opened the floodgates of sadism, and although the present-day Butchers, Exterminators, and Destroyers have long since surpassed him in clinical detail, Spillane's perception of violence remains readily identifiable: "I rolled on top of him and took that head like a sodden rag and smashed and smashed and smashed and there was no satisfying, solid thump, but a sickening squashing sound that splashed all over me" (*My Gun Is Quick*). He had from the start a talent for stirring up bloodlust through hard-driving prose. The reader is made constantly aware of "the thrill of running something down and pumping a slug into it."

In the world of Spillane's anarchic private eye, everything reduces to a Manichaean struggle between the essentially solitary Mike Hammer and a shadowy inexorable network of moral monsters whom it is his mission to destroy. Society and its elected representatives enter the picture only as forces seeking to deter Hammer from the fulfillment of his mission. It's all terribly ironic—the liberal do-gooders who object to Hammer's violent methods will never understand that he is protecting them from an evil that he alone can fully grasp. With the police Hammer has a love-hate relationship. He despises them when they kowtow to corrupt politicians or allow their hands to be tied by legal scruples, but acknowledges that fundamentally they fight the good fight.

Spillane's novels have a curiously dreamlike atmosphere. Many things happen, but none seems particularly substantial; the sole reality is Hammer's consciousness, which is propelled by an apparently continuous sense of thwarted rage. This inchoate anger echoes like a litany on page after page: "Maybe it was just me, but suddenly I wanted to

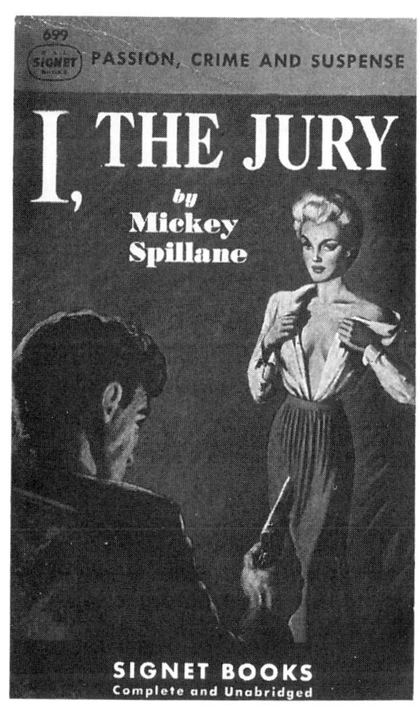

Signet 699 (1948)
Artist: Lou Kimmel

Signet 888 (1951)
Artist: Lou Kimmel

grab that guy in the overcoat and slam his teeth down his throat and wait to see what his two boys would do" (*One Lonely Night*); "I loved to shoot killers. I couldn't think of anything I'd rather do than shoot a killer and watch his blood trace a slimy path across the floor" (*Vengeance Is Mine*); "I hate the guts of those people. I hate them so bad it's coming out of my skin. I'm going to find out who 'they' are and why and then they've had it" (*Kiss Me, Deadly*). Psychology becomes indistinguishable from physiology: "I was just one tight knot of muscle, bunched together by a rage that wanted to rip and tear" (*My Gun Is Quick*).

There could also be drawn from Hammer's musings a compendium of by now familiar dicta on such topics as Communists ("So I was a sucker for fighting a war. I was a sap for liking my country. I was a jerk for not thinking them a superior breed of lice!"—*One Lonely Night*); lesbians ("She was another one of those mannish things that breed in the half-light of the so-called aesthetical world"—*Vengeance Is Mine*); and gun control ("If the D.A. wants to jug me . . . I'll throw the Constitution in his face. I think one of the first things it says is that the people are allowed to bear arms"—*Vengeance Is Mine*).

Beyond that, Spillane is a supremely professional storyteller, a master at encouraging the reader's identification with his avenging hero. The original cycle of Mike Hammer novels, beginning with *I, the Jury* (1947) and culminating in *Kiss Me, Deadly* (1952), made him a genuine superstar of fiction writing. Hammer sold more books than Sam Spade and Philip Marlowe put together: in 1953 New American Library boasted that "over 15,000,000 copies of his books have been published in Signet editions." His fans wanted—and got—such extra flourishes as Spillane's signature on the back cover, and photographs of the T-shirted novelist posing with his dogs and his arsenal of firearms. He even went so far as to appear in a movie, playing himself in *Ring of Fear* (1954). Years later he would get around to playing Mike Hammer in *The Girl Hunters* (1963), but by then the more urbane—if equally violent—James Bond had replaced Hammer as hero figure.

In fact, as far as the movies were concerned, Hammer never really clicked, although Robert Aldrich's *Kiss Me, Deadly* (1955) was a brilliantly abstracted black-and-white nightmare that reveled in the underlying paranoia of its source material and turned it into an unforgettable evocation of atomic terror. Other efforts to film Spillane fell flat; audiences may have realized that the books' main selling points—orgasmic violence ("His teeth came out in my shoe") and not-quite-orgasmic sex ("Her body was a milky flow of curves under the translucent gown")—would never survive translation to the screen.

So Spillane's triumph represented the triumph of the paperbacks as well. They were on the limit of the permissible, far beyond movies and television and radio. In that respect their only real competition was the girlie magazines then beginning to make their impact. To liberal intellectuals, Spillane was a symbol of the most terrifying aspects of American culture, and his fantastic success a vindication of their worst fears. Paperbacks had been lauded initially for bringing Shakespeare and Homer and Thornton Wilder to the masses, but those were evidently not what the masses wanted to read.

Even Philip Marlowe was appalled. In his pallid final outing, *Playback* (1958), Chandler's hero indulged in an uncharacteristic literary-critical interlude: "I picked a paperback off the table and made a pretense of reading it. It was about some private eye whose idea of a hot scene was a dead naked woman hanging from the shower rail with the marks of torture on her . . . I threw the paperback into the wastebasket, not having a garbage can handy at the moment."

John D. MacDonald similarly acknowledged Mike Hammer's influence in *The Neon Jungle* (1953), making him a principal character in the daydreams of the small-time embezzler Walter Varaki: "The bed lamp made a bright light on the book he was reading . . . It was the second time he had read the book. He was reading faster than usual, so he would get to the place where Mike Hammer takes the big blonde up to his apartment. That Hammer! There was a guy knew how to live. They didn't mess with him. Not twice, anyway. He had what it took with women. He wasn't stuck in any two-bit grocery business . . . Walter Varaki slid into a more comfortable position and began to read hurriedly. He was Mike Hammer."

So must a lot of men have been. The apotheosis of Mike Hammer was reached with the remarkable "Girl Hunt" ballet in Vincente Minnelli's M-G-M musical, *The Band Wagon* (1953). An enormous Technicolor paperback fills the screen (its cover art an immediately recognizable parody of Signet's Spillane covers), and then parts to reveal Fred Astaire as the unlikely incarnation of the ultimate tough detective. The sequence, by fusing movie-musical aesthetics at their most self-consciously rarefied with a lyricized version of all the erotic and violent content of the Spillane novels, achieved the kind of tension and balance that can result from a wedding of opposites.

For their day the Mike Hammer novels were notably erotic, but it was a curious eroticism indeed. We are given—in *Kiss Me, Deadly*, for instance—the phenomenon of Hammer rapt in the contemplation of statuesque beauty ("The static current of flesh against sheer cloth made it cling to her in a way that made me hold my breath to fight against the temptation I could feel tugging at my body"), but the object of desire has a very slim chance of reaching the last page alive. There are good women and bad in the Hammer novels, but they all have one thing in common: a tendency to die violently. Most vivid are the culminating scenes in which, time and again, Hammer wreaks vengeance on the woman who is the ultimate source of evil, a woman who in those final moments is apt to be transformed into something else—a mass of scar tissue (*Kiss Me, Deadly*), or "a ghastly wet red mask that was really no face at all" (*The Big Kill*). "Mike, how could you do it?" asked one lovely temptress whom Hammer had just shot fatally. His reply became something of a legend: "It was easy."

Not that Spillane was alone in this. The images reproduced in this book testify to the frequency with which eroticism and violent death were equated. The desirable woman, if she is not a murder victim, is likely to be a murderess: *Dames Don't Care*, *Women Are Like That*, *A Dame Called Murder*, *Deadlier Than the Male*, *Savage Bride*, *The Devil's Daughter*, *This Woman Is Dangerous*. "As he looked at her torrid beauty, he knew she would bring him only shame and disaster, but he didn't care." These fictions offered to every repressed male in America the consolation that if he had indulged his desires, he probably would have found himself staring down the barrel of a .45.

Woman is the pivot around which swirls all the unease of the paperback novels. The novelists (and the copywriters) did their best to defuse the mystery and terror of woman, offering the reader "a lusty woman who knew what she wanted—and how she wanted it"; "a mink-coated blonde who wanted to get Reno-vated from her husband but not from his dough"; "a passionate, amoral wench"; "a woman so beautiful no man could leave her alone"; "a beautiful and willful girl whose unconventional behavior and amorous escapades made her name a byword from Harlem to Greenwich Village"; "a luscious little cutie from Dixie with a mind of her own"; "a cute blonde with a provocative gleam in her blue eyes"; or "a cute trick who if she were in the dictionary would be listed under 'sex appeal.'"

Here we have the reverse of the Romantic tradition. If the Woman venerated by the Romantics was featureless, dephysicalized, infinite, beyond definition, then the Dame of hardboiled fiction must be strictly corporeal, a bundle of clearly defined instincts, a limited being appropriate to a literary genre that is essentially concerned with limitation. When Edgar Allan Poe invented the detective story, it must have been a lifesaving device for him, a way to maintain that the tremendous

Dell 370 (1950)

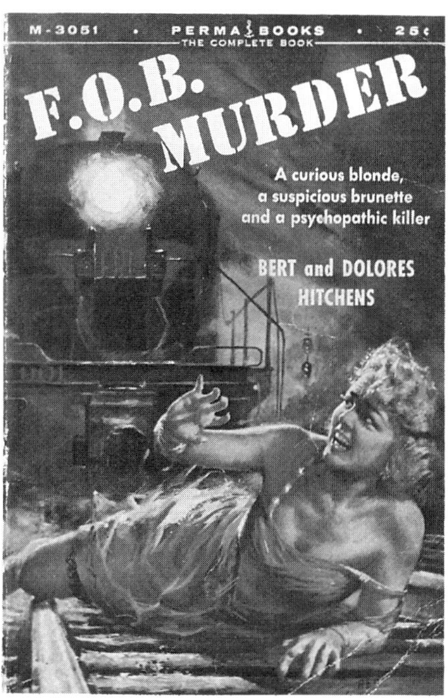

Perma M3051 (1956)
Artist: Robert Schulz

forces of horror within him, the rampaging orangutan, could be successfully brought to bay by the calm logic of an Auguste Dupin. Certainly Poe was the man in whom the Romantic notion of Woman had most thoroughly run its course, for whom an image like Keats' "Belle Dame Sans Merci" was no melancholy conceit but rather a nightmare he was unable to stop embracing.

Early detective fiction stayed in the safe, *Boys' Adventure* realm of *Treasure Island* and *20,000 Leagues under the Sea*, where the feminine principle, eclipsed, assumes the passive forms of ocean, island, grove. In the world of Sherlock Holmes, closed off to sexuality in the same way his Baker Street apartment is closed off to the rain and fog outside, mysteries are brought under control and reduced to objects: a stolen letter, a vial of sleeping potion, a hidden ventilation shaft. These are anomalies in an otherwise ordered world where time and space make a neat grid. By correlating a timetable and a map, it is a simple matter to isolate the disturbing element.

This kind of detective story excludes women for the same reason it excludes the supernatural: they are mysteries beyond the capacity of the detective. The presence of woman creates a problem which he cannot "solve" in his wonted fashion. A revealing exception is A. E. W. Mason's charmingly dated, mildly perverse *The House of the Arrow*, written in 1924, in which the well-bred young girl to whom the hero is initially attracted turns out to be a frenzied sadist. This solution permits the author, first, to spin out a very simple plot to book length, on the premise that "no one would ever imagine that the girl did it" (although the unchivalrous modern reader guesses this almost instantly); and, second, to fail to provide any motive for her string of crimes. Being a woman, she simply took it into her head, out of boredom, to become a murderess.

In the limited role he alloted to women, Dashiell Hammett in his early stories did not differ significantly from the Victorians. When, in *The Dain Curse*, the curtain lifts a little, it reveals a familiar figure:

> Gabrielle Leggett came around a corner just ahead of us. She was barefooted. Her only clothing was a yellow silk nightgown that was splashed with dark stains. In both hands, held out in front of her as she walked, she carried a large dagger, almost

Avon 564 (1954)

> a sword. It was red and wet. Her hands and bare arms were red and wet. There was a dab of blood on one of her cheeks. Her eyes were clear, bright, and calm.

It is Ligeia and Berenice and Madeline Usher come back from the tomb again, this time as a California cultist of the pre-Manson era. Another Hammett story, "The Scorched Face," also touches on a bizarre religious sect, and here, when it becomes a question of the sexual conduct of the converted, Hammett's style becomes uncharacteristically stilted:

> She cleared her throat, and started again, staring down at her feet. . . . "Hador was a devil. He told you things and you believed them. You couldn't help it. He told you *everything* and you believed it. Perhaps we were drugged. There was always a warm bluish wine. It must have been drugged. We couldn't have done those things if it hadn't. Nobody would—He called himself a priest—a priest of Alzoa. He taught a freeing of the spirit from the flesh by—" Her voice broke huskily. She shuddered.

The hardboiled style, which can take all manner of beatings, shootings, knifings, and garrotings in stride, is at a loss when confronted with unleashed sexuality. Suddenly we are back in the world—and the prose—of Victorian ghost fiction. (For that matter, a story like Joseph Sheridan Le-Fanu's "Carmilla" is franker in its eroticism than most hardboiled writers.) Hammett is on surer ground with the prostitute Dinah Brand in *Red Harvest*, but she must be killed to satisfy the demands of the plot. She is the most vital person in the book, and her death is consequently inevitable. With her vanishes the fleeting possibility of a happy sexual relationship, something that would strike at the heart of the genre.

If the detective surrenders to sex, he loses his powers. He must be a permanent voyeur, watching everything with detachment. In Chandler's *The Long Goodbye*, Philip Marlowe has a close brush with desire that sends him running for the whiskey (in lieu of cold shower):

> . . . Putting my arms around her I touched bare skin, soft skin, soft yielding flesh. I lifted her and carried her the few

> steps to the bed and lowered her. She kept her arms around my neck. She was making some kind of a whistling noise in her throat. Then she thrashed about and moaned. This was murder. I was as erotic as a stallion. I was losing control . . .
>
> I went back to the door and shut it—from the outside this time. Some kind of weird noises were coming from the woman on the bed, but that's all they were now. Weird noises. The spell was broken.
>
> I went down the stairs fast and crossed into the study and grabbed the bottle of Scotch and tilted it. When I couldn't swallow any more I leaned against the wall and panted and let the stuff burn in me until the fumes reached my brain.

All in all, this is not too different from Spillane, except that Mike Hammer would hardly have let himself be deterred by Marlowe's kind of scruples. Again, in an early (1954) John D. MacDonald thriller, *Area of Suspicion*, the hero engages in similar furious combat with a temptress, this time in mind only as he speeds away by car from her devouring embrace:

> All my desire for Niki came burning and torrenting upon me, spewing into my mind all the erotica of the solid, steady, metronomic surging of her hips while her eyes rolled wild and all of her was supple in her torment and her breasts were burning hardness, and her arms grew awesomely strong, and her broken mouth was lost in a demented babbling, keening and mewling between the whistling gasps that measured, by their frequency, her desperate climb to her peak of urgency. All the bright hotness of her in my mind, coming so strongly and suddenly, brought an icy sweat that soaked my body, and brought a knotted aching tension to my loins, and made me too sick and dizzy with my need to be able to drive.

This particular siren turns out to be a Communist agent rather than a Satanist, for all the difference it makes. Plainly these beings belong to another order of reality, and their "weird noises" and "keening and mewling" mark their separateness from ordinary humankind.

Popular Library 192 (1949)
Artist: Rudolph Belarski

Questions of sexual identity naturally enough compound the anxiety. During decades when homosexuality was barely a blip on the radar screen of mainstream culture, crime fiction had found a variety of uses for lesbian and gay male characters. For Dashiell Hammett, for instance, a character like Joel Cairo in *The Maltese Falcon*, with his "short, mincing, bobbing steps" and "round, effeminate chest," provides another shading for the book's gallery of exotic types; his identity as homosexual is subordinate to his identity as a *Levantine*, that is, a repository of every form of vice and Oriental rascality. Nevertheless he is not represented as a threat to civilization or even to the composure of Sam Spade. His main role is to be the butt of a series of rough jokes, to say "Oh, you big coward!" when Spade threatens him, or to cry out "as a woman might have cried" when punched in the mouth by his lover, the gunman (and gunsel) Wilmer, in an episode which elicits from Spade a grin and a derisive remark about "the course of true love."

Spade's bullying may seem indistinguishable from that of Mike Hammer, but there is a difference. Spade treats Cairo with amused contempt, but he sees his homosexuality as a foible in the same general category as the promiscuity of Brigid O'Shaughnessy or the womanizing of Miles Archer, a venial rather than mortal sin. There are none of the squeamish undertones which rise increasingly to the fore in subsequent decades.

Raymond Chandler's Marlowe affects something of the same indifference: "He was like Caesar," Marlowe says of the murdered pornographer in *The Big Sleep*, "a husband to women and a wife to men. Think I can't figure people like him and you out?" In his letters Chandler made clear his fundamental discomfort with the subject, affecting a certain humane tolerance but declaring, for example, that "homosexuals (not bi-sexuals, that is a matter of time and custom), however artistic and full of taste they may seem to be, always lack any deep emotional feeling," and speaking of "the peculiar mentality of the homosexualist, his sense of taste, his surface brilliance often, his fundamental inability to finish anything." (Coming from Chandler, a chronic procrastinator who in later years left many projects uncompleted, this is quite amusing.)

James M. Cain, in *Serenade*, plunges into the midst of the territory that Chandler nervously skirted. This novel, dedicated to the bold proposition that there is "five percent of a homo in every man, no matter how masculine *he* imagines himself to be," centers on the dilemma of a near-great opera singer caught between two figures who represent the poles of his sexual nature. His singing ability goes up and down like a yo-yo depending on which pole dominates: Winston Hawes, the rich and brilliant invert who by seducing him robs him of his gift, or Juana, the earthy, illiterate Mexican prostitute who restores not only his manhood but his singing voice. Homosexuality is here identified with civilization, while Juana, with her erotic healing power, represents a Rousseauan state of nature. Hawes is pretty much Chandler's homosexual —brilliant surface and emotional hollowness—decked out in more elaborate accoutrements. He is fabulously wealthy, able to manipulate the hero through far-flung economic and political influence; he is the most aesthetically advanced musician in the world, though there is "something wrong about the way he thought about music, something unhealthy"; he is, naturally, pallid and fine-boned, to contrast with Juana's dark-skinned, broad-hipped earthiness. When Cain wants to find a metaphor for Hawes' fundamental evil, he can only compare him to a woman: "He was like some woman that goes to concerts because they give her the right vibrations, or make her feel better, or have some other effect on her nitwit insides."

Winston Hawes can be taken as a paradigm of the homosexual stereotype that becomes more visible in the forties and fifties: a member of a social elite, wielding hidden influence even though his proclivities are in conflict with those of mainstream society. He is not merely personally subversive; he is part of a larger conspiracy. In *Serenade*, as elsewhere, the gay subculture is seen as a grotesque carnival: "A whole mob of them was in there, girls in men's evening clothes tailored for them, with shingle haircuts and blue make-up in their eyes, young guys with lipstick on, and mascara eyelashes, dancing with each other too, and at least three girls in full evening dress, that you had to look at twice to make sure they weren't girls at all." The individual may be risible; the *mob* is terrifying.

The terror was never more rawly expressed than in Mickey Spillane's *Vengeance Is Mine* (1950), a raging variant on *I, the Jury*. In the earlier book Hammer falls in love with a beautiful lady psychiatrist who turns out to be the leader of a dope ring and incidentally the murderer of Hammer's best friend. Mike responds by shooting her in the stomach while she is performing a seductive striptease in an effort to dissuade him. In *Vengeance Is Mine* this episode is constantly recalled as the great romantic tragedy of Mike's life, the reason why he hesitates to get involved with model agency executive Juno Reeves, even though she affects him powerfully: "Her smile made sunshine and the funny feeling started around my stomach."

Juno—"queen of the lesser gods and goddesses"—is a remote, regal beauty whom Mike feels constrained to put on a pedestal, even as she tells him that "I think I like to be treated rough and you're the only one who has tried it." She invites him to dinner at an "unusual" little restaurant which he knows well as "a fag joint." There, despite his slight unease at the surroundings ("There was a pansy down at the end of the bar trying to make a guy who was too drunk to notice. . . . I got a smile from the guy and he came close to getting knocked on his neck"), they continue their coy courtship, flirting, holding hands, but never quite getting down to business.

It comes as little surprise that the imperious Juno turns out to be the mastermind of yet another criminal ring, and that Mike will close in for the kill in the last chapter, Luger in hand. But memories get in the way and he can't do it: "I didn't think it would be this much trouble to kill another woman but it is." The impasse is resolved when Mike, grappling with the fleeing Juno, accidentally tears her gown off: "Damn it, I knew it all along and it was too incredible to believe. Me, a guy what likes women, a guy who knows every one of their stunts . . . and I fall for this. . . . I knew why I'd always had a resentment that was actually a revulsion when I looked at her. Juno was a queen, all right, a real, live queen. You know the kind. *Juno was a man!*" Since Hammer cannot, this time around, kill a woman, she must be transformed into a man: "I forgot all my reservations about shooting a woman then. I laughed through the blood on my lips and brought the Luger up as Juno swung around with eyes blazing a hatred I'll never see again." It feels like a ritual slaughter, with the victim killed in order to preserve the hero's faltering sense of equilibrium.

The tough-guy hero holds up well enough under the third degree but, as we have seen, he is apt to turn to jelly at the hands of a woman. There lies his frailty, which differentiates him from the archaic heroes who were equal to every kind of experience: when he comes to the male/female nexus, it is as a brick wall to him. He cannot look on the other side of it, because to do so would risk destroying his identity as hero, might plunge him into a chaos where the hard line dividing good and evil would blur. His line of descent is through Crusaders and Puritans; a woman can teach him nothing; he is lost if he enters too deeply into her mind. It is not the wisdom of self-knowledge but the anxiety of self-control that governs his conduct. He is in effect (appropriately for the age) a frightened hero. At the moment when he draws back from the plunge into chaos, he has a sudden glimpse of his monstrous other self: it is the face of the murderer. "This was murder." So Marlowe pours down the whiskey, trembling at how close he had come to being the object of his own investigation. Like a Parsifal warding off bewitching maidens with the sign of the cross, Marlowe brandishes his shot glass.

And they are indeed insubstantial enough, these women, to dissolve convincingly into mist. They are a mosaic of brightly colored molecules, clustered together to make a pliant lifelike form. The surface wavers and invites, but if you break the surface, the form dissolves. She cannot in any real sense act; she can only manifest all the attributes of the icon. Miss Harriet Huntress, in Raymond Chandler's "Trouble Is My Business," is as formalized a figure as any Medieval saint or Ainu fire goddess:

> She wore a street dress of pale green wool and a small cock-eyed hat that hung on her ear like a butterfly. Her eyes were wide-set and there was thinking room between them. Their color was lapis-lazuli blue and the color of her hair was dusky red, like a fire under control but still dangerous. She was too tall to be cute. She wore plenty of make-up in the right places and the cigarette she was poking at me had a built-on mouth-piece about three inches long. She didn't look hard, but she

> looked as if she had heard all the answers and remembered the ones she thought she might be able to use sometime.

Never having existed, she is indestructible. Prose—at any rate in the hands of a writer like Chandler—can evoke her even more surely than can the cover painting of dress and eyes and makeup and cigarette. The painting, fixing the form, seems somehow to diminish the reality of what was never anything but a floating wraith made of words. When you are dealing with a transcendent category, it is best to show as little as possible; silence and concealment create the illusion. H. Rider Haggard's She was never more convincing than when hidden behind a veil. When we go back to the memorable hardboiled heroines, it is usually to find that they consisted merely of a couple of gestures, a couple of lines of dialogue, a couple of brief vivid tableaux.

They are not what would be called "interesting characters"; they have no psychology, only perversity, like the heroine of Dashiell Hammett's "Fly Paper": "There was nothing in the Hambleton history to account for Sue, the youngest member of the clan. She grew out of childhood with a kink that made her dislike the polished side of life, like the rough. By the time she was twenty-one, in 1926, she definitely preferred Tenth Avenue to Fifth, grifters to bankers, and Hymie the Riveter to the Honorable Cecil Windown, who had asked her to marry him." Useless to look for anything but "a kink." The eyes are saying nothing, just a bare blank edge. The "character" is composed of absences.

The extreme example is Gloria, the death-haunted Hollywood extra in Horace McCoy's *They Shoot Horses, Don't They?* She, too, is no character; she represents a borderline of the human personality, beyond which it cannot be said that there is a person there. She lost most of her mysterious power when incarnated by a flesh-and-blood Jane Fonda. Gloria is an icon, beyond motive or explanation. But she is quite definitely *there*.

> "Why don't you quit the movies?" I asked.
>
> "Why should I?" she said. "I may get to be a star overnight. Look at Hepburn and Margaret Sullavan and Josephine Hutchinson . . . but I'll tell you what I would do if I had the

> guts: I'd walk out of a window or throw myself in front of a street car or something."
>
> "I know how you feel," I said; "I know exactly how you feel."
>
> "It's peculiar to me," she said, "that everybody pays so much attention to living and so little to dying. Why are these high-powered scientists always screwing around trying to prolong life instead of finding pleasant ways to end it? There must be a hell of a lot of people in the world like me—who want to die but haven't got the guts—"

She has the looks and lingo of a comfortable hometown girl, but Gloria is really a serene vampire in love with nothingness. She is the coolest of the cool, the solid crystal shape that remains when a hundred gaudier figures have been reduced to their essence: the frail, alcoholic women of David Goodis; the morbid ghosts of Cornell Woolrich; Chandler's sullen, murderous blondes; the lost girls of Ross Macdonald. McCoy's dry temperament enabled him to see the haunting image plain. Gloria is Poe's Woman, Coleridge's Life-in-Death, standing for once clear of the murkily sensual aura cast around her by a Romantic death wish.

The girl standing there chewing gum in broad daylight on Wilshire Boulevard is the Angel that remains in the wake of the male rejection of woman: a creature without desire, infinitely pure because her mind is fixed on death alone. The hero, having fled from the embrace he perceives as monstrous and engulfing, moves unerringly to a rendezvous with the unearthly woman who invites him to death.

Such deathly assignations were given prominent expression in the film noir, the Hollywood genre that developed later but eventually ran parallel with the hardboiled novel and its offspring, the trashy paperback. An atmosphere of Germanic doom surrounded the alluring will-o'-the-wisps incarnated by Lizabeth Scott (*The Pitfall*), Jane Greer (*Out of the Past*), or Yvonne De Carlo (*Criss Cross*). The blonde phantom in the rain; the glittering woman at the next table whose face reveals nothing; the woman with a secret, on the run from some undiscoverable dark past—they represent all that is other, the world beyond appear-

Popular Library 120 (1946)

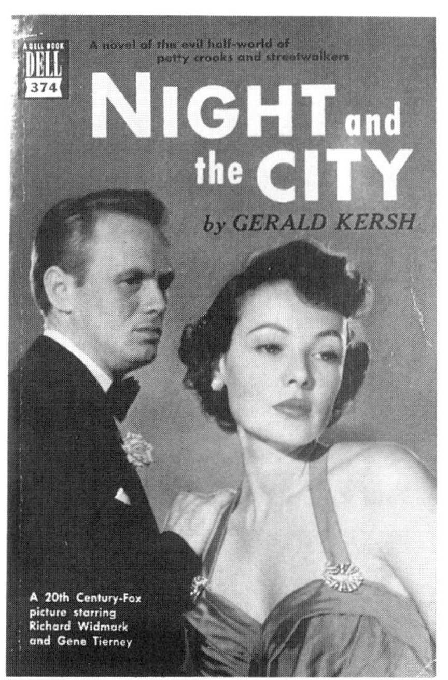

Dell 374 (1950)

ance. Veronica Lake, with her pallid, fragile features that expressed everything and nothing, became an image of freedom, of escape from limitation. The escape was into death, whether actual (in gun battle or car crash) or symbolic (flight to a tropical haven, a "new life" in a vague paradise beyond the horizon). Again and again, Hollywood took the hardboiled novel and turned it into *Tristan and Isolde* among the racketeers.

In picking over the source material provided by Hammett and company, the various media of the day seem each to have found a different angle to emphasize. The paperbacks had the sex, thanks to the First Amendment and to the absence of restraints like F.C.C. rulings and the Hays Code. Radio characteristically played up the comedy: Sam Spade and Philip Marlowe lost most of their toughness when they hit the airwaves and became easygoing quipsters with a penchant for jokes about martinis. (But there were exceptions—the Fifties program *Broadway Is My Beat*, for instance, invariably featured a number of poetic excursions in the lyrical/tough vein, rueful little monologues backed up by car honks and some mournful saxophone, that seemed always to begin: "It was autumn in the city . . .")

The movies, in the Forties at any rate, took a more romantic approach. The dry, hard texture of James M. Cain's novels was softened into the Germanic shadows and elegant eroticism of Billy Wilder's *Double Indemnity* and then into the out-and-out mush of Tay Garnett's *The Postman Always Rings Twice*. (Hollywood had waited too long on *Postman*. The book had been considered unfilmable on moral grounds for years, and when it was finally made, the era was all wrong. What should have been a clipped 80-minute Warner Brothers crime picture became a long, lugubrious M-G-M weepie.)

On the whole, Hollywood and the hardboiled novel had a good give-and-take relationship. A good deal was lost to typecasting, blue-penciling, and studio-dictated endings (for instance, the killer in *The Big Sleep* should have been Martha Vickers, not John Ridgely), but these minor betrayals were compensated for by a visual poetry that did justice—and often more—to the original works.

As for the scripts, critics at the time complained about their banality, but in retrospect the late Forties, as far as the crime film is concerned, seem like a Golden Age. Most of the novelists discussed in this book also functioned as screenwriters, although usually on versions of somebody else's book, so that William Faulkner adapted Raymond Chandler (*The Big Sleep*), Jonathan Latimer adapted Dashiell Hammett (*The Glass Key*) and Kenneth Fearing (*The Big Clock*), and Raymond Chandler adapted James M. Cain (*Double Indemnity*). (Dashiell Hammett's lone screenplay, a slavishly faithful adaptation of Lillian Hellman's *Watch on the Rhine*, is not in the running.) Not infrequently, the screenwriters managed to improve even on the best source material; one need only consult the last reel of *The Big Clock* and compare it to Kenneth Fearing's astonishingly casual resolution of an otherwise taut novel.

What Hollywood mainly had to offer was the greatest collection of visual and dramatic talent then in existence, and the means for them to exercise their talents to the fullest. Especially since the rise of Fascism in Europe, the studios had become an extraordinary international gathering place for directors, cinematographers, musicians, set designers, costumers. It was the Europeans who demonstrated the greatest flair for film noir—Robert Siodmak (*Criss Cross*), Billy Wilder (*Double Indemnity*), Otto Preminger (*Fallen Angel*), Andre de Toth (*The Pitfall*), Edgar Ulmer (*Detour*), Jacques Tourneur (*Out of the Past*), Jean Renoir (*The Woman on the Beach*), Max Ophuls (*The Reckless Moment*), and, above all, Fritz Lang, who seemed as if born to transmit his glacial visual impressions of America in films like *The Woman in the Window*, *Scarlet Street*, *The Big Heat*, *Human Desire*, and *While the City Sleeps*. Something in Lang's *Weltanschauung* clicked with America's uneasy reckoning with the forces of evil. His movies are at once alien (so alien as to seem almost extraterrestrial) and of the everyday—the bright, ordinary sidewalks, burger joints, and police stations of a banal and terrifying America.

Lang's Gothic vision blended almost imperceptibly with what was becoming a large-scale tendency. The titles tell the story: *The Dark Mirror. So Dark the Night. Somewhere in the Night. Scarlet Street. Nightmare Alley. Dark Passage. I Walk Alone. Kiss of Death. Force of Evil. In a Lonely Place. Where the Sidewalk Ends. On Dangerous Ground. Dark City. Shockproof. Ruthless. Panic in the Streets. The Killer Is Loose. Crime Wave*. Hollywood was definitely hooked on darkness, perhaps in hommage to the black-and-white movie as it gave way to Technicolor. As it turned out, film noir was too wedded to the chromatics of black and white to survive the transition to color. Color demystified the rain-slick midnight streets and the smoky nightclubs. That whole shadowy universe was drained of its poetry as by the coming of dawn in a city.

The femmes fatales and atmosphere of operatic doom found in movies like *Out of the Past* and *The Strange Love of Martha Ivers* were naturally transmuted into the primary-color language of the paperback covers. In place of leisurely swirling camera movements and high-contrast play of light and shadow (not to mention the vibrant histrionics of Barbara Stanwyck or Gene Tierney), the paperbacks offered a cruder but more compact image. The villainous Clara of David Goodis' *Behold This Woman* became, in Bantam's 1948 edition, a statuesque black-gowned creature, the face remotely modeled on Barbara Stanwyck's, posed against a pink satin bedspread, glancing obliquely at a mirror adorned with a carved Cupid, while the usual faceless male stares at her, fingers writhing in a paroxysm of some dark emotion. The copy announces simply: "SHE DESTROYED FOUR MEN." The artist responsible for this cover, William Shoyer, went one better a year later for the Lion Books edition of *The Devil's Daughter* by Peter Marsh. In keeping with Lion's more sensational approach, the woman's breasts double in size, her position is half-reclining rather than standing, and the man's fingers clutch an automatic. The jacket copy undergoes a similar metamorphosis: "SHE DESTROYED SIX MEN—WOULD HE BE THE SEVENTH?"

As always, the paperbacks had the advantage of being able to borrow whatever they needed from Hollywood, while at the same time remaining free to go beyond Hollywood's limits of decorum. Often the borrowing was above-board: the movie tie-in was an early marketing ploy, sometimes in the form of a publicity photograph in lieu of cover painting, sometimes (unthinkable to today's advertising strategists) an artist's independent "interpretation" of a scene from the movie, with a 50-50 chance of the actors' features being recognizable. In general, the movie-

Bantam 407 (1949)
Artist: William Shoyer

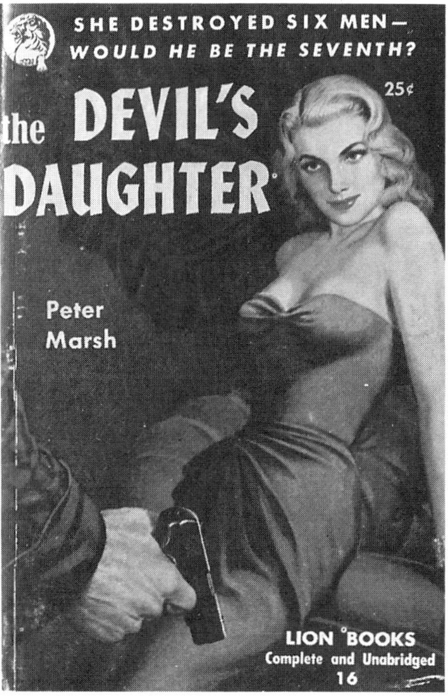

Lion 16 (1949)
Artist: William Shoyer

A double cross blew their chance for a million-dollar pay-off!

The Asphalt Jungle

W. R. Burnett

COMPLETE AND UNABRIDGED

Pocket Books 714 (1950)

tie-in covers were among the least interesting, since they took for granted an excited response that in other cases had to be created out of nothing, without benefit of Richard Widmark or Rita Hayworth.

There was a fairly close connection between the stylistic cycles of the movies and those of the paperbacks. Just as the book covers evolved in the early Fifties away from the heavy solidity of oils toward jazzy ink and pencil lines, so the movie melodramas of the late Forties gave way to a sparer, tougher kind of action picture along the lines of *The Asphalt Jungle*, *The Enforcer*, and *The Killing*, with their rapid-fire cutting and flat, bleached look. The background music changed, too—from the symphonic sweep and rich schmaltz of a Max Steiner to the jangling, insistent staccato of Leonard Bernstein's score for *On the Waterfront*. Witty repartee faded out as heroes became ever more blunt and thuggish. Violence escalated rapidly: man kicks old lady in wheelchair downstairs (*Kiss of Death*); man throws scalding coffee in girlfriend's face (*The Big Heat*); man is killed by cutting cable of elevator he is riding in (*The Garment Jungle*); man pushes pregnant girlfriend off roof (*A Kiss Before Dying*); man tortures wife (*Valerie*); man threatens to kill small child (*The Line-Up*); man kills small child (*The Phenix City Story*). By 1956, Hollywood had caught up with Mickey Spillane.

Most significantly, women were now to play a very secondary role. The dominating, larger-than-life figures associated with Stanwyck and Crawford and Tierney pretty much vanished from the crime film (although they found occasional refuge in off-the-wall Westerns like *Johnny Guitar*, *Rancho Notorious*, and *Forty Guns*). Women were relegated to being anonymous girlfriends and housewives, powerless victims (Esther Williams in *The Unguarded Moment*), or small-time floozies (Gloria Grahame in *The Big Heat*). The idea of a tough hero abandoning everything for the love of a beautiful temptress had lost its credibility; the new heroes were far more concerned with their struggles for supremacy over other men. The woman stood on the sidelines while the central conflict was being enacted between man and man. The lecherous villain of yesteryear began to metamorphose into a psychotic woman hater; the woman held hostage by the bad guy was now more likely to be tortured than seduced. Something had turned very sour.

In the mass art produced in that period, the image of woman is omnipresent—obsessively so—but it is an image drained of life. She has hardened into pure icon. In the crime films, she is often pawn, prize, hostage, or victim; only rarely is she independent actor. As if to signal this transformation of person into object, the focus of male sexual feeling passes from the face to the breasts. Voyeurism reigns: it is not the exchange of amorous glances that excites, but the secret stare of the peeping tom. (This tendency was to surface in a run of early Sixties movies revolving explicitly around the voyeur—*Psycho*, *Look In Any Window*, *Experiment in Terror*.)

In the Forties, the paperback covers often seemed like crude imitations of movie scenes. In the Fifties, on the other hand, the movies themselves often seemed like strings of paperback covers—flat, bright, violent surfaces devoid of character but brimming with emotion.

Each of these surfaces—movie poster, film frame, cover painting, page of text—tries to be more than surface, to bring the viewer or reader into immediate contact with a reality more real than the place where you (watcher or reader) are standing. You approach those surfaces as if to enter the genuine place, the place where the action is. It is a quest for an impossible kind of directness, an image or event so unmistakably *there* that you need not even a split second to analyze or question it.

They fail to deliver, of course, although if the movie moves quickly enough you may not notice. As for the cover, it proposes a mystery more curious than a writer could resolve. It is the perpetual teaser, the open door beyond which is no room, no house, no place at all. We follow where it leads, and are inevitably disappointed. But the beckoning image is still there, ever open and enigmatic, like the bold red question mark that flashed from many a paperback mystery.

The text is the innermost chamber we can reach by passing through the inviting surfaces. The words are the edge of the real; beyond them there is only the blank page. And the words do try to reconstitute the dreamed-of immediacy: "He ran up the stairs." "There was a crash." "Then he saw her." The words are laid out like markers, so that the page is the room, is the street, in which the words move like human beings. The text wants to be so immediate that it escapes from language altogether and becomes action.

Yet at the heart of this attempt, something odd happens. The hardboiled novel—which is meant to be concerned with action, with dialogue, with the complicated and dynamic interrelationships of people and places and times of day—that perpetually humming machine tends in fact toward a zero state of silence, solitude, and immobility. If we remove the temptresses and gunmen, we are left with a drab room in which a man alone smokes many cigarettes and empties many bottles of Scotch.

It is no secret that a large percentage of the hardboiled writers were alcoholics—yet another quest for immediacy. Tobacco and alcohol provide a bass line underlying the high flights of action. Anyone who has read Hammett, Chandler, and the rest while trying to give up smoking is painfully aware of the cigarette as punctuation mark. The smoke that lingers in the rooms of these fictions serves as a ritual incense to invoke the proper mood of expectancy. Consider Sam Spade's office in the first chapter of *The Maltese Falcon*:

> On Spade's desk a limp cigarette smoldered in a brass tray filled with the remains of limp cigarettes. Ragged grey flakes of cigarette-ash dotted the yellow top of the desk and the green blotter and the papers that were there. A buff-curtained window, eight or ten inches open, let in from the court a current of air faintly scented with ammonia. The ashes on the desk twitched and crawled in the current.

Raymond Chandler had evidently learned his Hammett by heart when he embarked on the opening of "Trouble Is My Business":

> I watched her shake ash from the cigarette to the shiny top of the desk where flakes of it curled and crawled in the draft from an open window.

The Bull Durhams and Fatimas of Hammett's operatives have long since passed into legend—as indispensable to a detective as trenchcoat and automatic. The smoking and drinking also provide an occult link between writer and reader. One envisions the reader sipping his whiskey and puffing on his Lucky Strike while reading a description of a hero busying himself with those identical activities, as transcribed by a writer who was likewise engaged.

The typical hardboiled detective novel is structurally similar to cycles of heavy drinking: exhilaration and depression alternate predictably. The recurrent descriptions of the hero recuperating from a severe beating may owe much to the author's memory of his most recent hangover. For the public all this imbibing was part of the rollicking merriment which came to be associated with detective novels. In Jonathan Latimer's parodistic books (*The Lady in the Morgue, The Dead Don't Care*), whiskey drinking is the central activity, occasionally interrupted by the plot. Hammett's *The Thin Man* takes advantage of its Christmas-to-New Year's timetable to allow the consumption of innumerable cocktails. For Hammett, this forced gaiety was to be his final word, followed by decades of apparently depressed silence, while Nick and Nora Charles maintained independently their career of carefree besottedness.

It is sometimes difficult to determine the extent to which parody was intended. For instance, in Paul Cain's Hammettesque *Fast One* (1932), a random five pages yields the following:

> Cullen went into the kitchen and came back with tall glasses, a bowl of ice and a squat bottle . . . He opened his eyes, sat down and poured two drinks. . . He sipped his drink, leaned back . . . Kells put his glass down . . . Kells picked up his glass, drained it, stood up . . . Cullen was pouring drinks . . . Cullen was stirring his drink . . . Kells nibbled at his drink and stared out the window . . . Cullen was stirring ice into another drink . . . Kells finished his drink, picked up his hat and put it on . . . He picked up his drink . . .

For the solitary hardboiled hero, smoking and drinking have nothing to do with having fun; they are spiritual activities akin to the motionless sitting of the Zen monk. The detective is never more himself than when he is apparently doing nothing at all. Paul Pine, in John Evans' *Halo in Brass* (1949), provides a casebook illustration of the action hero as contemplative:

> I leaned against the window frame and looked out and thought my thoughts. I lighted a cigarette and bounced the folder of matches on my palm . . . I put them in my pocket, went over and mixed another drink and carried it back to the window.
>
> I stood there a long, long time. Dusk slowly filled the street below and began to crawl in at the window. The sky lost its hot look and became a soft faraway gray. A red neon sign in a haberdashery across the way came on and threw a harsh pattern of color across the walk . . . I moved my coat off the bed, pushed up the pillows and stretched out with my glass and a cigarette and a mind filled with drifting thoughts . . .

No fears about smoking in bed for such a man. Like most of the derivative private eyes, he is able to mimic the moves of a Philip Marlowe, but without a trace of the real despair that hovers around Chandler's creation: "I seemed to hear a steady ticking somewhere, but there wasn't anything in the house to tick. The ticking was in my head. I was a one-man death watch"; "I was as hollow and empty as the spaces between the stars" (*The Long Goodbye*).

In that light the booze and cigarettes are a handrail that the detective, finally alone and separated from his narrative, grasps to keep himself from the void that stretches beyond it.

Curiously, the tolerance of heavy drinking rarely extends beyond the hero himself. In all other characters drinking is usually an indication of weakness or depravity, as can be seen in the staggering number of staggering heiresses, mistresses, wives, and rich widows (not to mention dim-witted rummy hirelings with the shakes) that drift through the literature. If the author wishes to go one step further, to underscore the stereotype, the alcoholic temptress becomes a user of opium, marijuana, or cocaine, while the hireling's DTs are transformed into junk sickness. By feeding his villains drugs rather than drink, the writer has radically increased their distance from the hero.

Narcotics of one kind or another figure rather prominently in the history of detective fiction, but despite the example of Sherlock Holmes, with his predilection for morphine and cocaine, they are generally associated with the forces of evil. The prevalence of drugs in the mystery novels of the early twentieth century can perhaps be attributed to their wide over-the-counter availability. In 1929, a few years before the Federal Narcotics Bureau succeeded in imposing its worldview, Hammett's Continental Op (in *The Dain Curse*) could still take a fairly level-headed view of the ravages of addiction:

> ". . . What's your day's ration?"
> "Five—ten grains."
> "That's mild enough," I said, and then, casually: "Do you like using the stuff?"
> "I'm afraid it's too late for my liking or not liking it to matter."
> "You've been reading the Hearst papers," I said. "If you want to break off, and we've a few days to spare down there, we'll use them weaning you. It's not so tough."

In earlier fiction the drugs most frequently resorted to are opium, morphine, and cocaine. Marijuana and hashish were either less notorious or not taken seriously enough to warrant inclusion. It took the great American antihemp crusade of the early Thirties to turn marijuana into a worthy subject matter for sensational fiction. It was a rapid process of education. As late as 1932 Cab Calloway could cavort (in Paramount's *International House*) to the strains of "Have You Seen That Reefer Man," presumably to the innocent bewilderment of most of the American public. By 1936 the situation was getting clearer, although Jonathan Latimer's description of a group of musicians getting stoned in the back room of a restaurant is considerably more lighthearted in tone than the massive propaganda campaign then in full swing:

> . . . Smoke as thick as fine gray silk sheeted the back room from ceiling to floor, eddied around a peach-colored electric bulb, made indistinct the silent figures of men grouped about a central table . . .

Crane shook his head, kept his eyes on the men, who smoked in silence, apparently unaware that anyone had entered the room . . .

"Don't worry 'bout them guys," said the waiter, loudly. "Don't even worry a little bit. They ain't on the same plane with us . . . They're bein' absorbed . . . See that guy on the table? Well, he's Bray-mer. He's doin' the absorbing . . . Those other guys," he stated, "they're undergods. But they ain't on the same plane with Bray-mer yet. They gotta keep smokin' to make it. . . ."

As he rose to leave Crane asked Udoni how he happened to be mixed up with the cult in the next room.

"Those are my boys," said Udoni. "Many musicians have cults, as you call them. It makes the dreams beautiful, instead of sordid, as they ordinarily are from marihuana. I myself rarely smoke, but now it helps me . . . forget."

"You mean you get so you really believe in Brahma?" Crane demanded.

Udoni said, "After the second cigarette one believes anything." (*The Lady in the Morgue*, 1936)

Shades of Fusion Music and the New Age! But the facetious Latimer was hardly the man to appreciate the full seriousness of marijuana. It took a paranoid of the order of Cornell Woolrich to do full justice to the drug's dangers, as in this episode of an innocent girl who finds herself alone with yet another jazz musician:

. . . She could see the mistrust starting to film his face, cloud it over. It was coming up fast, almost like a storm, behind his eyes. Behind it in turn was something more dangerous; stark, unreasoning fright, the fright of drug-hallucination, the fright that destroys those it fears . . .

She'd had no experience with marihuana-addicts before; she'd heard the word, but to her it had no meaning. She had no way of knowing the inflaming effect it has on emotions such as suspicion, mistrust and fear, expanding them well beyond the explosion-point, providing they are latent already in the subject . . .

She wasn't talking to a man, she was talking to the after-effects of a narcotic. (*Phantom Lady*, 1942)

Chandler's Philip Marlowe—never one to condone decadence—took a slightly less hysterical although equally unsympathetic view:

> "Anybody can smoke reefers," I said. "If you're dull and lonely and depressed and out of a job, they might be very attractive. But when you smoke them you get warped ideas and calloused emotions. And marihuana affects different people different ways. Some it makes very tough and some it just makes never-no-mind . . . Quite possibly all three murders are connected with the reefer gang." (*The Little Sister*, 1949)

Up until the 1950s, marijuana and drugs in general were just part of the general freak show, a subsidiary manifestation of the central many-tentacled Evil, like male homosexuality, lesbianism (see John Evans' luridly uninformative *Halo in Brass*—or, for that matter, Graham Greene's *Stamboul Train*), and, at times, intellectualism (Spillane again). But by 1953 things were changing. A note of realism enters the descriptions of pot smoking, which multiply dramatically. Jazz musicians are still taking the rap, of course:

> . . . Gus's car was moving so slowly. It had taken them hours merely to travel these few blocks. But everything else was creeping too. The other cars seemed not to be moving, but to be suspended at a succession of advancing points. Never before had he realized the distinction. And Gus was talking, beautiful, meaningful, at times hysterically funny things he was saying, and in reply there was giggling, his own . . .
>
> "Charge, now, man, it's a funny thing about smoking charge," Gus said as they drove on. "It usually takes time . . . I mean, you gotta know what kick it is you're looking for, you know? But sometimes a cat makes it the very first time, like you did, man . . . yeah!" (Douglas Wallop, *Night Light*, 1953)

But the picture is expanding. These hip-talking, pot-smoking musicians who have been appearing regularly for the last twenty years as a comical sideshow or as homicidal brain-damaged berserkers are seen now not to be alone. There is a world out there that the paperback novels begin to fill in piece by piece. There are, for example, the inner cities:

> . . . She got out a match flap and ripped the unused matches from it, scattering them so that the wind carried them across the roof of the tenement. She doubled the empty cover backward and put the butt of her cigarette in the fold to make a crutch. She took another drag, hissing in the smoke, letting it out slowly.
>
> If Dolores wanted to take a tea ride it was her own private affair. Chico had tried it more than once himself. But with Dolores somehow it was different. She never did anything just for kicks. Most of the time she was so quiet, so intense, but now and then she had the jumps bad. Chico didn't know what to make of it—muggles didn't hit you that way. Muggles made you cocky, sure of yourself. (Wenzell Brown, *Run, Chico, Run*, 1953)

And, it was beginning convincingly to be suggested, nice kids from good homes were doing it, too—kids like the one John D. MacDonald describes getting her first lesson in reefer smoking:

> "No, honey, you're not doing it right. Look. Like this. You put the cigarette in the corner of the mouth. See? But you got to leave your lips a little open so air comes in along with the smoke. Then you suck the smoke and air right down deep into your lungs. That's the kid! Come on. Again, now. That's the way, honey."
>
> . . . It was funny how fast it slowed the world down. She remembered how she could look at the speedometer and it said eighty, but looking ahead she could see every crack and pebble on the pavement, and it was as if she could hear the tick and thump of every cylinder in the motor . . .
>
> They'd ended up there, the four of them. Floating. The music was something that was new in the world. Notes like the slow ripple of silver cloth. All dim up there . . . Time went all crazy. It would drag and then speed ahead. There was the music. Teena floated. There was just one dim bulb and the music . . . Fitz gave her another stick and she went far away then . . . (*The Neon Jungle*, 1953)

This kind of material was not lost on the Gathings Committee of 1952. After scourging the paperbacks for their propagation of "sexual deviations and perversions probably before unfamiliar to the type of reader who now buys them," such as "homosexuality, lesbianism, and other sexual aberrations," the committee found time to signal another danger:

> Other paperbound books dwell at length on narcotics and in such a way as to present inducements for susceptible readers to become addicts out of sheer curiosity. As an example of how this subject is handled by current books, one need only read *Marijuana Girl*, by N. R. de Mexico (Universal Publishing and Distributing Co.). A more appropriate title would be: "A Manual of Instructions for Potential Narcotic Addicts."

Not bad, Congressman—but will it sell?

A year later Ace Books published, as side A of one of its Double Novels, a work entitled *Junkie: Confessions of an Unredeemed Drug Addict*, by William Lee. It was billed as frank and uncensored—and it was, so much so that Ace found it necessary to supplement the original text with footnotes contradicting the outrageous assertions made by the author, who was of course none other than William S. Burroughs incognito. If the footnotes were not enough to offset the book's plainly subversive message, the text on the flip side was there to set things straight: *Narcotic Agent* by Maurice Helbrant ("Gripping True Adventures of a T-Man's War Against the Dope Menace"), which proved on closer inspection to be a reprint of an exceedingly dull book originally published in 1941, amusing only for the unconscious play on words concealed in its title. The covers of this double volume tended to obscure the difference between junkie and cop. On Burroughs' book we are shown a frenzied male (presumably the future author of *Naked Lunch*) seizing a lovely blonde girl about the throat, as she grasps the hypodermic lying on the table in front of her. The companion cover depicts a male hand (belonging, one assumes, to the stern T-Man) putting the cuffs on a lovely brunette girl whose stylishly short hair may or may not have something to do with her being a dope fiend.

25c COMPLETE • UNABRIDGED POPULAR LIBRARY

DOCUMENTARY THRILLER

"This book is a documentary set down with the drama and pace of a thriller. Its villains are drug peddlers at home and abroad, its heroes the Federal agents who wage a ceaseless war against them."

Buffalo NEWS

In boxes labeled "machinery," in the secret rooms of ocean liners, in bandages, brassieres and hollow crutches, dope worth millions crosses American borders. School girls prostitute themselves for a "fix," honest men turn gunmen to support "the habit"—while "pushers" prosper in a deadly racket. Can America survive the international dope conspiracy? Here is the answer in a challenging, courageous book that sounds the battle cry against the underworld.

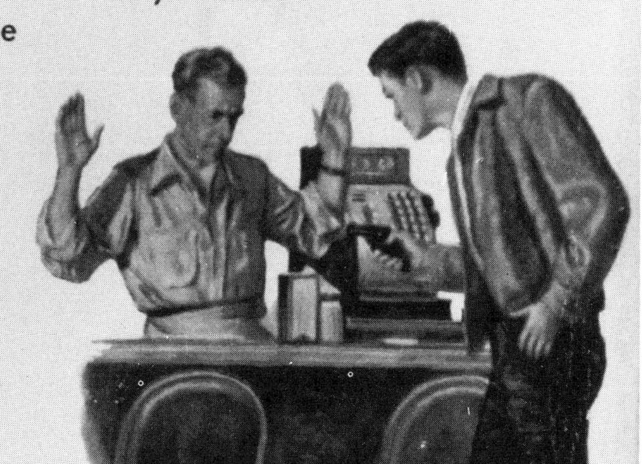

PRINTED IN THE UNITED STATES

Popular Library 528 (back cover)

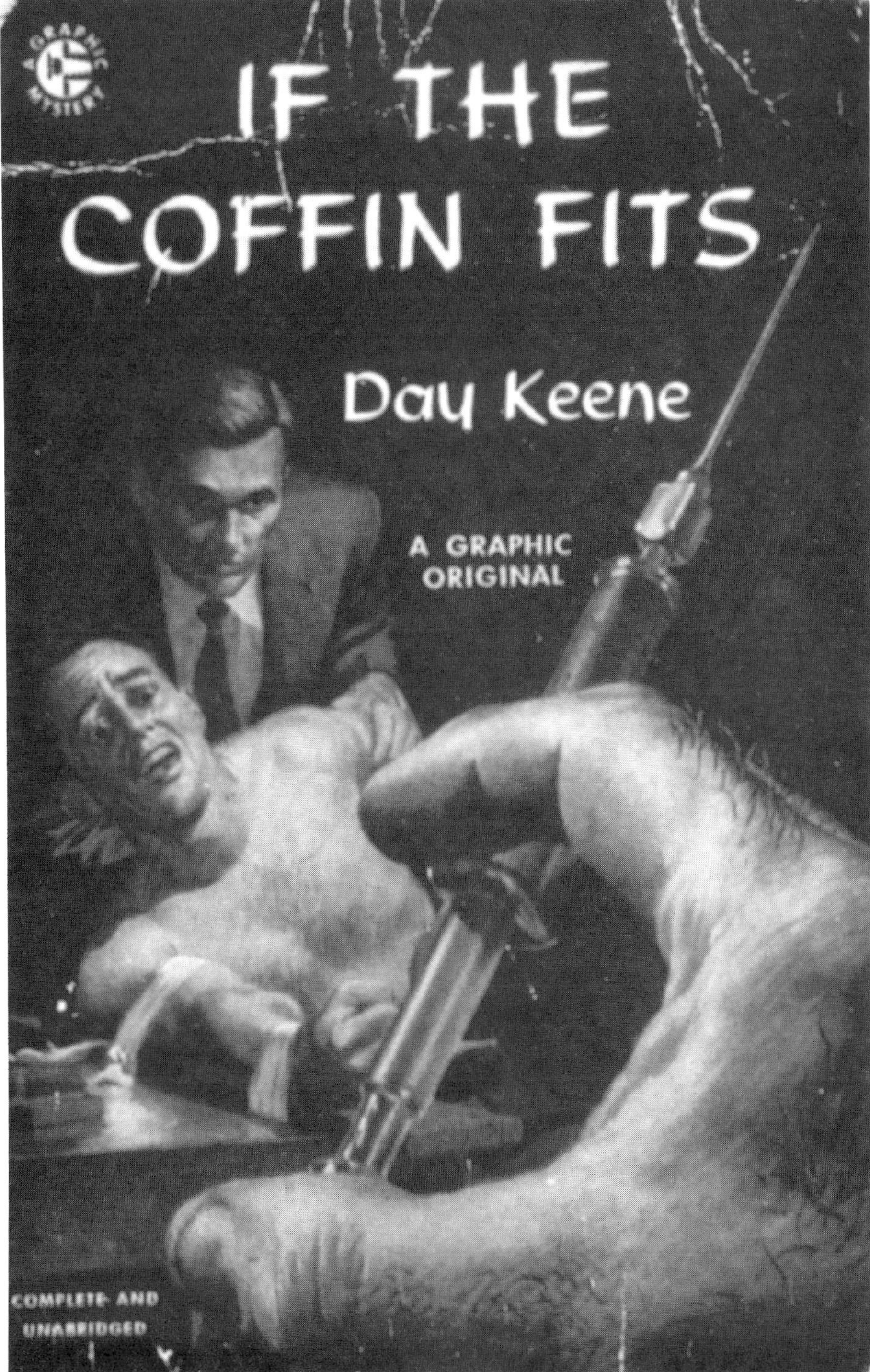

Graphic 43 (1952)

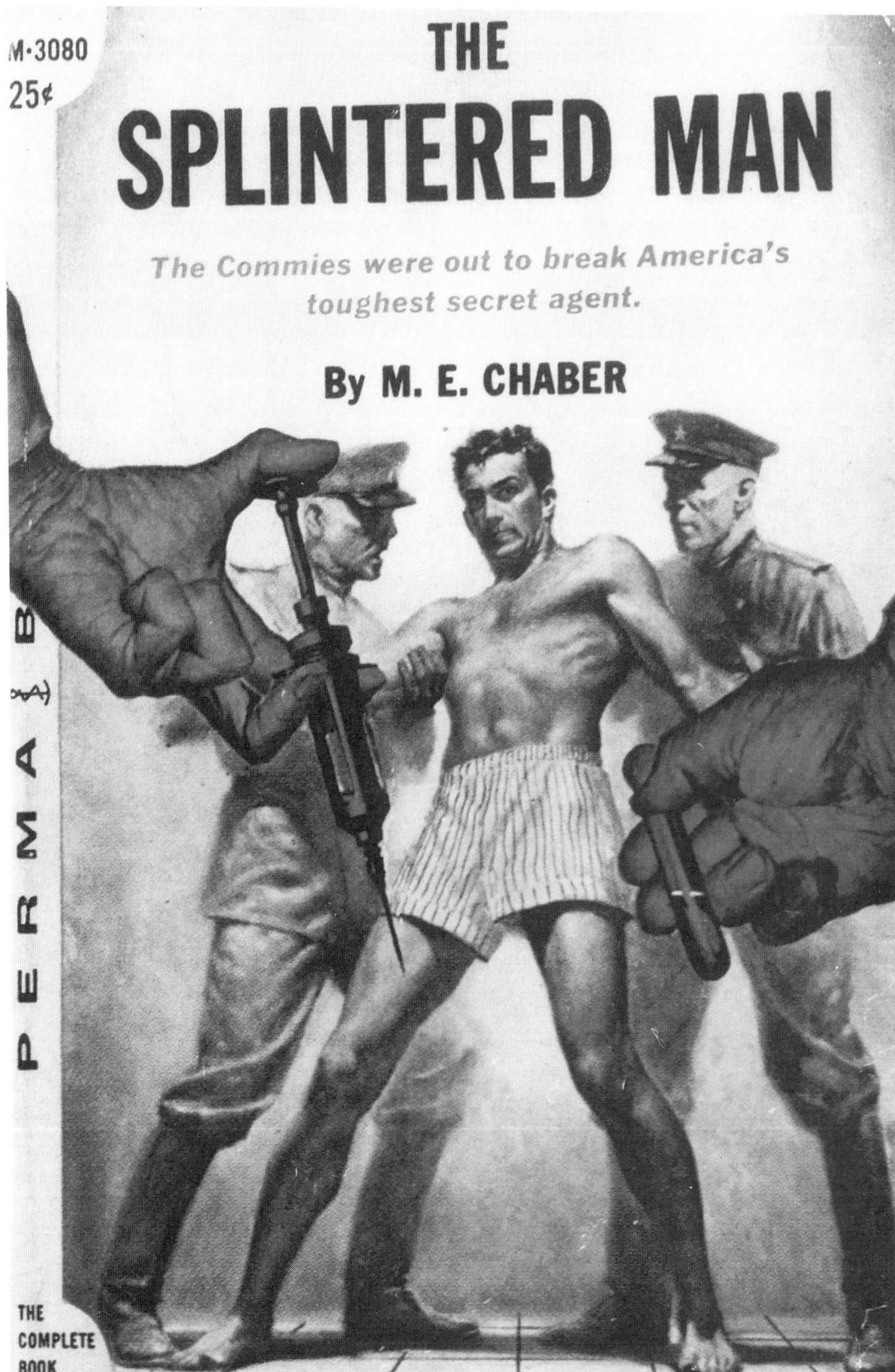

Perma M3080 (1957)
Artist: Robert Schulz

As if that were not enough, M. E. Chaber's *The Splintered Man* (a spy thriller published in 1955 and later reprinted by Perma Books) gave hints of even stranger things to come, as an American CIA agent submitted to chemical ordeals at the hands of an East German scientist:

> He poured water into the glass. He took a small metal case from his pocket and extracted from it an eye dropper.
>
> "This, gentlemen," he said, "is lysergic acid diethylamide. Fifty micrograms, fifty millionths of a gram, to be exact. As you can see, it is such a small amount as to be almost invisible. Yet this is a large enough dose to put the patient into a schizophrenic state for seven to eight hours."

In short order the hero succumbs to the drug's effects:.

> The colors were beautiful. Great arching streamers of color, shooting up in front of my closed eyes and bursting into brighter colors. Like the fireworks on the Fourth of July. Only prettier . . . I was really floating away from my body and how would I ever manage to get back to it? I tried swimming through the air, but my arms were back down there on my body. I was going to be lost out in space forever. It I didn't have my body, nobody could see me and they'd never be able to find me . . . My voice hurt from the screaming. I was doing the screaming, but I wasn't. It was a me that had nothing to do with me. A me away from me.

After all, it was only twelve years before the Summer of Love. On balance, no one in America—no one who kept up with the paperbacks, that is—could fairly say that there had been no warning.

Chapter Six

Afternoons of the Fifties

By the early Fifties, the private eye had pretty much run his course. There had been too many episodes of *The Fat Man* and *The Whistler* and *The Adventures of Sam Spade*, too many low-budget second features exploiting the same handful of plot devices, too many white trench-coats, too many plugs for Wildroot Cream Oil. Even Alan Ladd wasn't playing detectives any more. As for old-fashioned favorites like *The Pink Umbrella Murders* or *The Roman Hat Mystery*, they were ripe for the kind of parody being introduced by *Mad* magazine. Mysteries, which had (according to Frank Schick's history of paperbacks) constituted over half of all paperbacks published in 1945, had fallen to 26 percent by 1950 and to only 13 percent by 1955. In their place was a new sort of book, the paperback original. This was not a mystery in the classical sense, although you could count on an ample amount of really tough violence. You could also count on as much sex as could legally be squeezed in—or at least the promise of such. This was mature adult reading. It was also streamlined reading, made to be devoured in one breathless sitting.

For this kind of material, you might have turned to Graphic Mysteries, to Ace Books (who often gave you two novels in one volume), to Uni-Books or Handi-Books or Carnival Books (if you were really desperate), or to Popular Library, once they started publishing novels like Jim Thompson's *After Dark, My Sweet* and John D. MacDonald's *Cry*

Hard, Cry Fast (both 1955). But you would have gotten the most gratifying results by turning to two lines offering unusually high standards: Lion and Gold Medal. Lion Books was, in its brief career (it lasted from 1949 to 1957, under the editorship of Arnold Hano), the most offbeat of paperback imprints. Best remembered for having published much of the best work of Jim Thompson (including *The Killer Inside Me*, *A Hell of a Woman*, and *Savage Night*) and some of David Goodis's most uncompromising novels, Lion also issued a string of notable titles by Edward Anderson (a reprint of the Depression era classic *Hungry Men*), Shirley Jackson (*The Lottery*), Robert Bloch (*The Kidnapper*), Fritz Leiber (*Conjure Wife*), Richard Matheson (*Someone Is Bleeding*), David Karp (the strangely neglected *The Brotherhood of Velvet*, a convincing paranoid vision of a world ruled by preppies), Robert Payne (*The Deluge*, a bizarre "reconstruction" of an apocalyptic story idea by Leonardo da Vinci), Day Keene (*My Flesh Is Sweet*), and R. V. Cassill (*Dormitory Women*).

Lion 216 (1954)

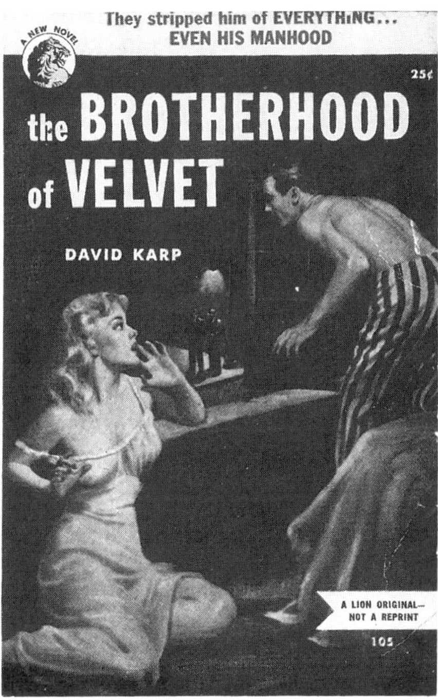

Lion 105 (1952)

But in the marketplace Lion was a fringe player, and could only aspire to the success of Gold Medal, the big winner of the paperback original era. Fawcett's Gold Medal Originals assured you that "THIS IS A GOLD MEDAL BOOK. Look for this seal when you buy a book. . . . The Gold Medal seal on this book means it has never been published as a book before. To select an original book that you have not already read, look for the Gold Medal seal"—unless, of course, it turned out to be a Gold Medal book that you had already read. But the thought was there.

A sense of déjà vu on the reader's part would have been understandable, given the predictable nature of Gold Medal's obsessions: *Hill Girl*, *House of Flesh*, *The Lusting Drive*, *Ripe Fruit*, *Homicide Hussy*, *Blonde Savage*, *Death Is a Lovely Dame*. But, unlike the product of such companies as Handi-Books and Graphic, Gold Medal's originals were frequently worth reading. Their authors—an astonishing roster—included David Goodis (*Street of No Return*, *Down There*, and many more), Cornell Woolrich (*Savage Bride*), Chester Himes (*For Love of Imabelle*, the first of the Gravedigger Jones–Coffin Ed Johnson novels), Richard Matheson (the legendary science-fiction novels *I Am Legend* and *The Shrinking Man*), Peter Rabe (tough-minded gangster sagas like *Benny Muscles In* and *A Shroud for Jesso*), Ann Bannon (now-classic Lesbian novels such as *Odd Girl Out*), Harry Whittington (a long line of sturdy narratives including *Fires That Destroy* and *Brute in Brass*), the ubiquitous Day Keene (*Murder on the Side* and many more), Louis L'Amour (*Hondo*), William Faulkner's kid brother John (*Cabin Road*), and Donald Hamilton (the Matt Helm series). Not to forget Theodore Pratt, whose much reprinted *The Tormented* (1950) featured what may have been the prototype of psychiatric seals of approval on "daring" books, in the form of a "Foreword by Richard H. Hoffman, M.D., Renowned New York Psychiatrist":

> This is an important book. It presents an authentic picture of nymphomania in a novel about a girl named Zona. It will be, no doubt, an enlightening, even educational experience for many to read this story of a girl who wanted to be a moral person and a good wife, but who found herself chained by insatiable, never-ending desire . . .

Aside from contributing to public enlightenment, Gold Medal also threw in a good deal of literary enlightenment. But if they published the odd masterpiece (and books like *For Love of Imabelle*, *I Am Legend*, and *Down There* certainly qualify), they also purveyed the most splendidly achieved of garden-variety genre novels, thanks in large part to the efforts of four of the most adroit plot-spinners of the paperback era: Harry Whittington, Gil Brewer, Day Keene, and Charles Williams. The work of these four—who were, it appears, good friends as well—exemplifies the way in which hardboiled fiction serves as the folklore of the technological age. Their novels are like traditional ballads, in which the same figures and elements recur endlessly, so that episodes might be transposed from one to another without the reader even noticing the difference. It is all part of the same eternal dream-life, in which the suitcase full of money goes from hand to hand and the sleepless hero grips the steering wheel ever more tightly.

Whittington has begun to enjoy a revival, proving that the relentless pacing and high-energy plotting of such novels as *A Ticket to Hell*, *Brute in Brass*, *You'll Die Next!*, and *Web of Murder* have lost none of their power to enthrall. Brewer's and Keene's books deserve to have their day as well, Brewer chiefly for the unmodulated intensity with which he works variations on the theme of seductive feminine evil (*13 French Street*, *Satan Is a Woman*), Keene for the sheer verve with which he lends credibility to even the most preposterous narrative conceits (see in particular, among his almost uniformly entertaining books, *Sleep with the Devil*, in which a professional killer conceals himself in a religious community).

Even more overdue is a wider appreciation of the work of Charles Williams, one of the most reliable of all the paperback professionals. Williams is at face value the epitome of a macho adventure writer. His heroes are characteristically preoccupied with hunting (*Hill Girl*), fishing (*River Girl*, *Go Home, Stranger*, *Girl Out Back*), athletics (*The Big Bite*, *A Touch of Death*), and, above all, with sailing (*Scorpion Reef*, *Aground*, *The Sailcloth Shroud*, *Dead Calm*). They are perfectly adapted to Williams's largely rural world, encompassing the gulf coast from Galveston to West Florida and the back country adjacent to it, a landscape of bayous and cottonfields, of stifling small towns and swamp backwaters thick with latent violence. When his characters talk about going to the big city they generally mean Shreveport.

Much of the charm of Williams's work derives from the affection he lavishes on his backgrounds. Even when his heroes are on the run with a suitcase of stolen money, they find time to watch the light sink into the foliage beyond the stream or to become absorbed in the silence of deep woods. The natural world stands in counterpoint to the dizzying and ultimately pointless human actions which Williams relates. This facet of his work is clearest in the sea stories, in which the presence of the sea is so vividly realized as to compensate for the occasional lapses in characterization. In *Dead Calm*, for instance, a climactic episode requires a wife to search for her husband across miles of empty ocean without a compass, relying only on a faint memory of how to navigate by the stars. Williams conveys with great intensity his sense of fragile human life somehow threading its way through a void, and he accomplishes this primarily by the extreme precision with which he describes the physical properties of the sea and the boat. It is a sort of romanticism expressed in the terms of *Popular Mechanix*.

Williams's first novels, the "Girl" trilogy (*Hill Girl*, *Big City Girl*, *River Girl*), made him one of Gold Medal's superstars. *Hill Girl* was one of the pioneering entries in the "swamp tramp" subgenre which flourished in the fifties. However, the eponymous hill girl is not the simple stereotype that Barye Phillips's cover art would suggest, and the novel itself—despite its familiar blend of hunting imagery, moonshine whiskey, barefoot country girl in cottonsack dress, shotgun wedding—is really about the hero's discovery that he knows nothing about women. The corollary of this is that he knows about men either—not even his adored brother, a reckless type whose profound psychosis emerges in an unexpected ending. *Hill Girl* is apprentice work but Williams's chief characteristics are already present: a powerfully evoked natural setting, revelation of character through sexual attitudes and behavior, and a conversational narrative voice that makes the flimsiest tale seem worth telling.

After hitting his stride with *River Girl*, an operatic account of doomed love which might be described as a male weepie, Williams was to concentrate for most of his career on a particular kind of plot. His

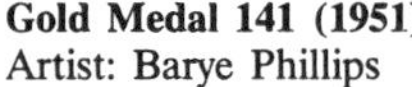

Gold Medal 141 (1951)
Artist: Barye Phillips

Gold Medal 286 (1953)
Artist: Barye Phillips

narrator is generally an ordinary, curiously amoral fellow fueled by greed and lust but curiously detached from his own crimes. *Hell Hath No Fury* (filmed as *The Hot Spot*), *A Touch of Death*, *The Big Bite*, *All the Way* (filmed as *The Third Voice*), and *Girl Out Back* are variations on the same serviceable plot: boy meets money, boy gets money, boy loses money. Each of them hinges on a woman, and it is in the intricacies of the man-woman relationship that Williams finds his real subject. Only occasionally (as in *A Touch of Death*) does he resort to that favorite film noir cliche, the mysterious murderous beauty. More often the woman is both more intelligent and—even when she is a criminal—more aware of moral complexities than the affectless hero, who is ultimately destroyed by his inability to read the woman's character, by his tendency to project a stereotype. The football hero of *The Big Bite*, probably Williams's best book, typifies this unraveling of single-minded toughness into gibbering paranoia.

This is not to say that Williams is interesting because of the obsessions and ambiguities implicit in his books. These would count for little without the strength of his narration, the ease with which he handles complicated intrigues, the constant sense of physical immediacy. He is not a writer like Jim Thompson, whose conflicts take him beyond genre altogether, forcing the reader up against the barriers of the fiction he is reading. In contrast, Williams always stays well within the parameters of a form predicated on satisfying the reader's expectations. The endings of *A Touch of Death* and *The Big Bite* are indeed open, like uncloseable wounds; the plot mechanism leads to an edge from which we can look into an abyss; but it is after all the character who falls into the abyss, leaving the reader safely behind to grasp the railing of structure. Not all of Williams's novels are of equal intensity—the relentless exploration of male character in the middle period gives way to a more conventional heroic stance in the later books—but from first to last he never deviates from the narrative values which make his books so entertaining and his present neglect so inexplicable.

And then—in a class absolutely by himself—there was Jim Thompson. Thompson broke most of the rules of crime fiction, or indeed any kind of genre fiction. A Thompson novel begins anywhere—inside a funereal barroom, a state penitentiary, or the mind of a psychotic—and ends nowhere. There may be two alternate resolutions, there may be none, there may not be enough of the narrator's personality (or indeed, as in *Savage Night*, of his body itself) left to tell us coherently what happened. Thompson's "heroes"—the homicidal sheriff Lou Ford (*The Killer Inside Me*), the amiable psychopath Doc McCoy (*The Getaway*), the misogynistic door-to-door salesman Dolly (*A Hell of a Woman*)—have trouble keeping their stories straight, since they lie not only to others but to themselves, and thus to the reader as well.

One wonders about those first readers who, in search of a few hours' undemanding escapism, picked up the Lion Books editions of *The Killer Inside Me* or *Savage Night* or *The Kill-Off*. Picture it: at the newsstand or the soda fountain, the casual browser's eye is caught by the lurid cover, the rapid-fire blurbs ("He Used Two Women to Feed His Brute Cravings") with their promise of a cheap and painless thrill, a tawdry but well-protected stopover in the lower depths. He begins to read, lured on by the compelling narrative voice with its folksy humor and jabbing emphases. Then—just as he thinks he is on the verge of finding the truth about the killing, or the robbery, or the kidnapping—he falls through Thompson's trapdoor. He's down in the depths, all right, not just the depths of the city but the depths of a mind, and no return ticket is being offered. The enthralling voice turns out to be the voice of someone who doesn't know who he is, who's no longer sure which story he's telling, who may have been lying all along. By identifying with this speaker (and Thompson's special gift is for forcing one to do just that) the reader inherits his curse: a psychic hell which goes around and around without ever arriving anywhere.

Anchoring the wilder reaches of these disintegrating protagonists is Thompson's rock-solid sense of place and of economic relations. The inhabitants of his world—pipeliners, elevator operators, small-time grifters, hit men, collection agents—confront their inner chaos within a hard-edged, undeniably real landscape of oil derricks and cheap hotels, warehouses and small-town jails and misbegotten taverns: "It was the kind of place where, if they didn't let you spit on the floor at home, you could go there and do it."

Thompson didn't start out as a crime writer. He came to it almost by default after decades of soul-crushing work ("hotel worker, plumber's helper, truck driver, pipeliner, routstabout and harvest hand," ran one blurb, not to mention bill collector, aircraft factory worker, gambler, vagrant, and director of the Oklahoma Federal Writers Project), and after trying his hand at writing of all sorts, poems, radio scripts, sociological reports, true crime stories, naturalistic fiction. The biographical realities underlying his fictional infernal machines remained obscure until the publication of Robert Polito's richly detailed *Savage Art*, which in telling Thompson's life also tells a significant chunk of 20th-century American history.

Thompson's first crime novel, *Nothing More Than Murder*, published in 1949 at the age of 43 after the commercial failure of two previous novels, already contains many of his standard ingredients: a homicidal hero who hides behind a stream of glib chatter, a tangled maze of anguished sexual relationships, and an elaborately detailed background—in this case the outer fringes of the film distribution business. By the time he wrote *The Killer Inside Me* (1952)—the first and still the best-known of his long string of paperback originals—Thompson had perfected his blend of outrageous humor, disturbing violence, and simmering identity crisis, all set against the landscape which was the extension of his vision: the epicenter encompassing Nebraska, Oklahoma, and West Texas. Thompson had begun as a regional writer—what else was an Oklahoman supposed to be?—but the apocalyptic images he extracted from the heartland were a far cry from any uplifting populism.

In many ways Thompson remained a political writer, although he could never have shared the systematic ideology of some of his colleagues in the Writers Project. The brilliant *Pop. 1280* is an overt travesty of racist demagoguery and institutionalized ignorance, and *Recoil* provides a prescient critique of a right-wing pressure group which more than slightly resembles Jerry Falwell's Moral Majority and all its progeny. Throughout his work a ferocious anger against exploiters and self-serving bureaucrats alternates with effortless compassion for the bums, the out-of-work, the rejects of capitalism.

Yet schematic political solutions can offer little to the denizens of Thompson's world. Their problems are rooted much deeper, not merely within society but within the family, within themselves, within the language they use to define themselves.

It's in his approach to language that Thompson's real originality surfaces. His books describe a space defined entirely by that unmistakable, omnipresent narrative voice. Even as he fills in the intricacies of his chosen setting, the narrator's voice is eating away at the carefully constructed reality. The voice starts out talking about the things surrounding it, but in the end only the voice remains. The protagonist of *Savage Night* loses even his body: "The darkness and myself. Everything else was gone. And the little that was left of me was going, faster and faster." Being itself erodes, right in front of us.

That's why filmmakers, who love to adapt Thompson's books, usually have to change the endings. There's just no way you can *show* the double narrative that closes *A Hell of a Woman*, the berserk fantasies of *Pop. 1280* and *Savage Night*, the death of the narrator in *After Dark, My Sweet*, and it would take a whole movie in itself to deal with the alternate world to which the fugitives of *The Getaway* get away. All along we thought we were in a real place and we end up—where, exactly?

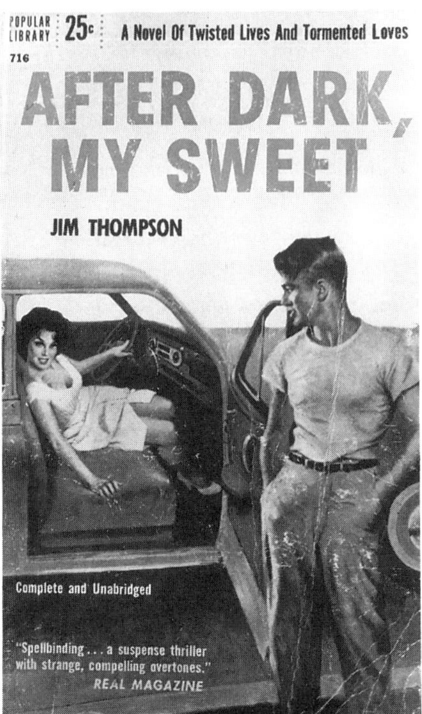

Popular Library 716 (1955)

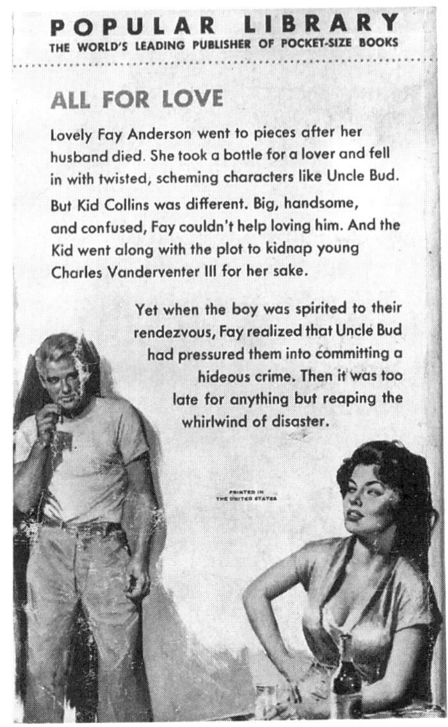

Popular Library 716 (1955) (back cover)

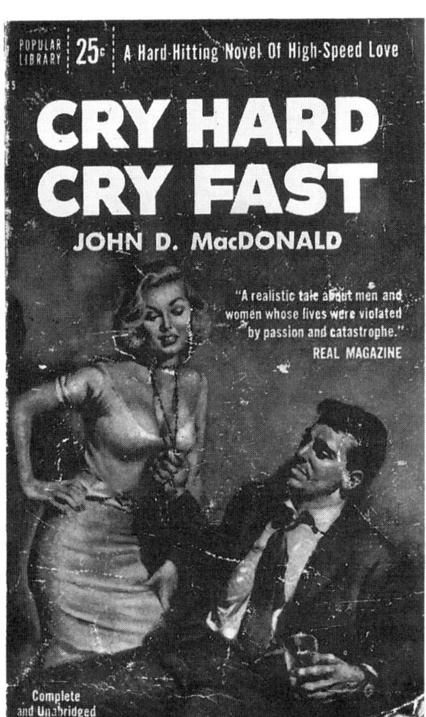

Popular Library 675 (1955)

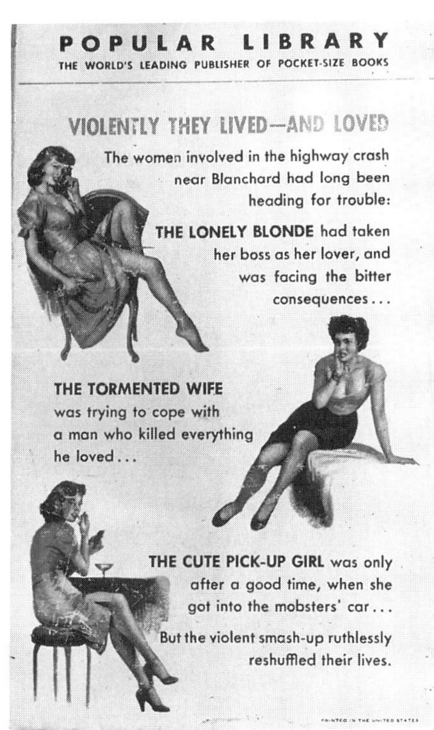

Popular Library 675 (1955) (back cover)

Thompson doesn't provide an answer: he just keeps asking the question, stripping away layers of personality, undercutting any sense of stability to get to the heart of his nightmare. We may well feel like the supervisor Thompson describes in *Roughneck*, unable to grasp that the company he's worked for all his life, with its tangible physical assets—"all the people 'n the buildings 'n the factories 'n the b-banks 'n the warehouses 'n the . . . the everything"—can somehow go completely out of existence: "Where—w-where the hell's it gonna be if it ain't there? What . . . where'n hell is anything gonna be?" The same incredulous horror informs all Thompson's books, right down to his novelization of the TV series *Ironside*, which evolves astonishingly into a vision of nuclear holocaust: "There would be no refuge from the coming terror. No familiar thing to cling to. Something would become nothing."

No familiar thing to cling to. The phrase describes perfectly the unnerving atmosphere of these novels. The hero of one of Thompson's last books declares: "I had tried to do right, whenever and wherever I could. But right and wrong were so intertwined in my mind as to be unidentifiable, and I had had to create my own concepts of them." More than one reader has finished *The Killer Inside Me* or *A Hell of a Woman* with a sense of having intruded on a personal struggle almost too painful for fiction. The narrator is not dramatizing the struggle between good and evil—he's living it, and the author is living it with and through him. Such naked internal conflict doesn't normally pertain to the literature of paperback escapism. We are closer to the mentality of a Dostoevsky, sharing the compulsion to expose moral ulcers, to acknowledge evil impulses, to seek some kind of redemption. But while Dostoevsky could come to rest in an image of religious orthodoxy, Jim Thompson remains out on a limb. There is no salvation, no point. Even when he tacks on a happy ending for the sake of the genre—as in *Recoil* and *The Golden Gizmo*—nobody is likely to be fooled. The pain underlying this work was not to be abolished by a stroke of the pen.

I am not suggesting that *A Swell-Looking Babe* or *Wild Town* are works as finished as *Crime and Punishment* or *The Possessed*. Thompson wrote rapidly and for money; his handling of plot and character grew increasingly perfunctory; he cheated on more than one ending. Yet what endures in his work is a relentless questioning, a moral intensity

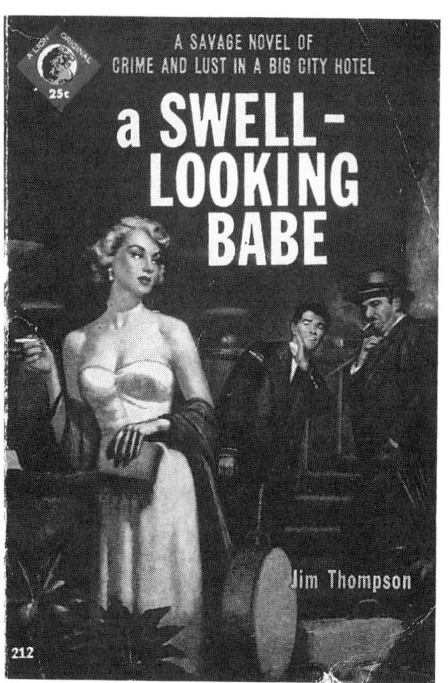

Lion 212 (1954)

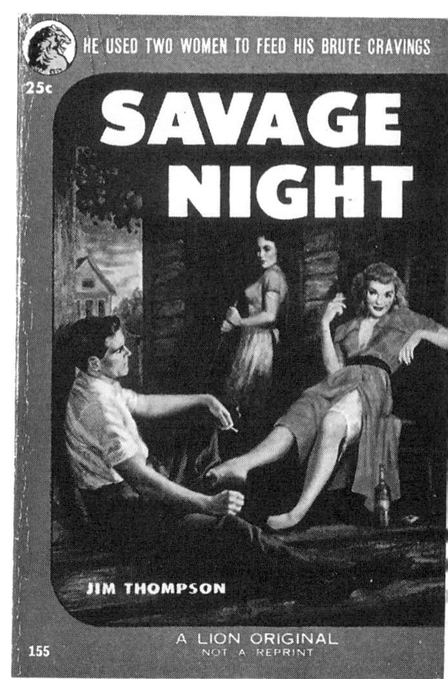

Lion 155 (1953)

unable to settle for an easy answer. We are always on the edge. Thompson might be, then, a dimestore Dostoevsky in a distinctly American mode, our very own underground man, choking on industrial fumes, blinded by neon bar signs, eking out a living as a door-to-door salesman or a third-rate con artist. A poverty of the imagination pervades his depleted, spiritless world: "The whole place had a kind of decayed, dying-on-the-vine appearance . . . There was something sad about it, something that reminded me of baldheaded men who comb their side hair across the top." Least of all is there any love. Sexuality consists entirely of violence, sometimes implied, usually acted out: hideous marriages begin in alcoholism and end in murder, joyless prostitutes fall prey to obsessive sadists. Rarely has an American writer—especially a mass market writer like Thompson—portrayed such hopeless ugliness, so unadorned a dead end.

The temptation is to read his books simply as testimonials of his own compulsions. Indeed, the recurrence of certain images—the murderous mother, the helpless father, the termagant wife, the terminally alienated, often impotent husband—invites such a reading. Yet although

Thompson's specific obsessions are personal, their *tone* belongs to the culture at large. His plot materials derive from the atrocities of the daily papers—he was, after all, a reporter and a regular contributor to *True Detective*—and his settings distill a lifetime's worth of highways and railroad yards and hotel lobbies. It's all too clear that, far from being subjective fantasies, Thompson's books faithfully reflect a mentality that seethes all around us, as American as the next mass murder.

Thompson, however, sees not only the violence of the murderer but the implicit violence of the social structures that shape him, the cannibalistic system of relationships within which he flounders, innocently bewildered. The horrors of the individual psyche are located within the organized horrors of state and church and family. Evil people, Thompson wants to say, have their own kind of warped innocence. They have problems too—they are just as confused, as put-upon, as self-pitying as the good people. These killers are not "villains"—they are helpless monsters, to be regarded with a kind of primitive awe. In daring to give literary expression to the most forbidden impulses, and to place them in a context which makes it impossible for the reader simply to condemn, Thompson perhaps told us more than we want to hear. We should listen anyway.

The star alumnus of the paperback originals—Gold Medal's greatest find—was John D. MacDonald, a publishing phenomenon still going strong years after his death, as his novels continue to be reissued for new generations. MacDonald proved himself from the start the kind of storyteller who makes other aesthetic considerations irrelevant. To read him is to hear a spoken voice—pausing, digressing, joking, all the while drawing you into the yarn. It's not that the story is so remarkable; you've heard something like it before, you may even recognize chunks of it from another of his books, and after a while, it will blend into all the others. The anecdote may be utterly banal. It's the *voice* that grabs you, the sure rhythms with which it measures out its story. And it can be any kind of story: MacDonald, a true all-rounder, tried his hand at science fiction (*Wine of the Dreamers*, *Ballroom of the Skies*); horror (*Soft Touch*); whimsical fantasy (*The Girl, the Gold Watch and Everything*); suburban soap opera (*Cancel All Our Vows*, *The Deceivers*);

bawdy comedy (*Please Write for Details*); true crime reporting (*No Deadly Drug*), not to mention a book about his pet cats (*The House Guests*).

What he started out doing was very much in the mainstream of Fifties paperback writing. Subsequently he went on to the more elaborate structures of *A Flash of Green* and *Condominium*, but many readers preserve a sneaking fondness for the swift, lean novels that preceded the advent of Travis McGee. They are considerably rougher and more pessimistic than the later novels. Reading them, one can envision one of those Fifties action pictures in black and white, something along the lines of Budd Boetticher's *The Killer Is Loose* or Joseph Pevney's *Female on the Beach*. *Dead Low Tide* (1953), *The Neon Jungle* (1953), *A Bullet for Cinderella* (1955), *Murder in the Wind* (1956), *April Evil* (1956), *The Price of Murder* (1957), *The Executioners* (1958)—they all seem to spring out of some long, hot American afternoon, an unfamiliar Cadillac gliding menacingly through the streets of a small town, a hundred tiny dramas of loyalty and betrayal, small lusts, quiet madness, interior dramas of regeneration, all set spinning about each other, meeting and meshing; and of that meshing a plot is born.

You may wince at the coyness of the lovers' dialogue, and find the subplots too neatly interlocked, but you can never doubt that MacDonald knows his America, his small town; especially if that town is located in Florida. The state is MacDonald's territory, and, from his novels could be extracted a long, lovingly precise litany of observed detail:

> Eighty-nine was a frame house that looked as if it had been picked up bodily out of some small Indiana town in 1914 and moved to Florida. Two stories and two stunted gables, and a deep front porch with rocking chairs, and brick front steps. That happens sometimes. People retire, and distrust the unfamiliar. So they come down here and duplicate the awkward living they have endured all the years of working and saving. Tired boxlike rooms and overstuffed furniture with crocheted dinguses on the backs and arms of the chairs. Ferns in pots, and two floors and an attic. There is a way to live in Florida—a way of turning a house inside out, so there is no real transition between outdoors and indoors. Glass and vistas and the good

> breeze coming through. Tile and glass and plastic, so there is nothing to absorb the dampness and sit and stink in dampness.
>
> But they come down and build their high-shouldered houses with the tiny windows, and thus what should be a good life turns into one long, almost unbearable summer in Indiana. (*Dead Low Tide*)

MacDonald's narrative mastery gives him the advantage of being able to digress as much as he likes. So sure is his control over the basic impetus of the story that he can throw in a grab bag of extras, discourse on his somewhat courtly sexual philosophy, analyze the decline and fall of Plymouth Gin, give practical tips on anything from caulking a houseboat to stopping a killer dog in its tracks to doctoring a set of books without breaking the law.

Through all this, there flutter traces of a political philosophy which remained (perhaps mercifully) indistinct, at least until McGee's sidekick Meyer let slip his admiration for the monetary policies of Admiral Pinochet. Early in his career, MacDonald perpetrated a few startlingly banal anti-Communist thrillers such as *Murder for the Bride* and *Area of Suspicion* (the latter subsequently reprinted only in an edition "specially revised by the author"), but many of his later books (notably *A Flash of Green*, *Pale Gray for Guilt*, *The Only Girl in the Game*, *A Key to the Suite*, *Condominium*) explore the vagaries of laissez-faire capitalism far more convincingly than most Marxist writers. MacDonald's magnates, racketeers, and crooked politicians are not fundamentally different in character from Hammett's or Chandler's, but we learn a great deal more about how they actually achieve and maintain their power. *Condominium* might almost serve as an instruction manual for aspiring land sharks. MacDonald is, after all, a graduate of the Harvard Business School, and all told he has probably taught more people the rudiments of capitalist economics than Milton Friedman and Paul Samuelson rolled together.

No use putting him in a category; MacDonald created his own identity, more garrulous than Cain, more full of color and joie de vivre than the monochrome paranoid worlds of Goodis or Cornell Woolrich. Not to say it's all cheerful going; readers of *The End of the Night* and *One*

Monday We Killed Them All know how rough MacDonald's sociopaths can play. The violence is fully comparable to that of any writer in the field. But there is always an element of measure, each book designed to contain a well-balanced set of ingredients as one would balance the ingredients of a meal, implying that MacDonald was not an obsessed man impelled to spell out the horrors of his vision; he was a professional, whose obsession was Narrative.

While John D. MacDonald was constructing his many-volumed chronicle of Florida, another Macdonald was beginning a similarly protracted study of the mores of southern California. Ross Macdonald had started out in the Forties writing (under his real name of Kenneth Millar) a number of rather tentative novels—although *Blue City* (1947) still holds up quite well—before turning definitively to his own variation on the classic private eye. The Lew Archer novels were attributed first to John Macdonald, then to John Ross Macdonald, before the emerging competition of John D. brought about the ultimate name change.

In his first outings, Archer appeared to owe a number of traits to Philip Marlowe—in particular, his style of repartee. Bantam Books did nothing to dispel the impression of a hardboiled romp with its Bogartesque jacket copy: "The name is Archer, Lew Archer, private detective in the land of dreams—California; in the land of peaches and honey, misery and murder—male and female! . . . If you stick a lighted match into a barrel of gasoline, something's going to happen, and as far as men are concerned that's what women are—a lighted match. Take the case of the Guilt-Edged Blonde or the Gone Girl or—but better yet, just turn the page . . ."

This radio-detective prose doesn't convey much of the quality of someone who toward the end of his career was praised more highly than any other mystery writer—too often, perhaps, by critics who combined their praise of him with backhanded swipes at the genre he worked in. The special appeal of Ross Macdonald's books to some may have been that he offered a nonviolent, liberal-humanist detective in sharp contrast to bloodthirsty hit men like Mike Hammer or The Executioner. Even the bad guys tend to be more cultured than the norm: the murderer in the first Lew Archer novel quotes Kierkegaard by way

Dell 408 (1950)

Pocket Books 907 (1952)
Artist: Clyde Ross

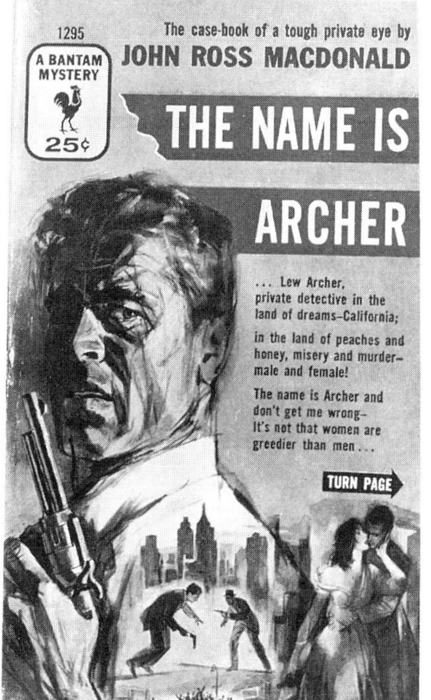

Bantam 1295 (1955)
Artist: Mitchell Hooks

Bantam 1360 (1955)
Artist: Mitchell Hooks

of self-justification, and poets and painters have figured prominently in subsequent books in the series.

With Lew Archer himself, Macdonald pulls off the neat trick of creating a character largely by negative means. Try to imagine him apart from the structure of the book and he becomes a cipher. We see through Archer's eyes, and react with him, but in the end he is little more than a window through which we perceive the real figures of interest—the people whom Archer is investigating. He is the interviewer, the neutral voice that calmly elicits anguished testimony. On one level, he is a brilliant dramatic device, a device that works because of Macdonald's mastery of dialogue. But he is also, when the going gets as rough and as weirdly twisted as it generally does, a kind of ballast that keeps the novel from falling apart when its characters begin to.

There is sleight of hand in all this, a skill necessary for a writer whose plots have a baroque splendor unprecedented in the genre. By comparison, Hammett's story lines were casual affairs, serviceable but not remarkable in themselves, while Chandler managed his transitions deftly but without fully masking the gratuitousness of his narrative structures. Neither ever surpassed in complexity or gracefulness the multigenerational mysteries of *The Chill* or *The Far Side of the Dollar*, books that approach formal perfection.

Macdonald's narratives are beautifully built machines in which the constructional genius of an Agatha Christie is wedded to a gift for writing about flesh-and-blood people in real and contemporary places. This particular combination of talents has not often, if ever, occurred in the mystery field (earlier on, it was declared an impossibility by Raymond Chandler in his essay "The Simple Art of Murder"). Many of Macdonald's plots would, if baldly summarized in proper chronological order and with all the confusions of identity laid bare from the start, appear as preposterous as *East Lynne* or *The Two Orphans*. Yet in practice they are not only believable, but moving. It is, in the best sense, a triumph of style.

Macdonald is able to make his structures work by resolving the problem first stated by Raymond Chandler in his discussion of Dorothy Sayers' work: "If it started out to be about real people . . . they must very soon do unreal things in order to form the artificial pattern required by the plot. When they did unreal things, they ceased to be real themselves." The classic whodunit ultimately fails to convince, because there is a single culprit and twelve or so innocent people, yet all must appear equally suspect until the last few pages. Inevitably this involves the manufacturing of a great many red herrings, particularly when (as is so often the case) the suspects are a random assortment of, say, guests at a weekend party.

In Macdonald's novels the shadow of guilt that flits from character to character is usually more than an illusion. He makes this credible by focusing on families and on the transference of emotional traumas within them. He often resorts to the same mechanics as the earliest detective stories. Can one really believe, for example, that a daughter could impersonate her mother so well as to fool half a dozen people, including the mother's lover? But the device works (in *The Wycherly Woman*) because the interrelationships of these characters are more than just a casual permutation.

Macdonald has been faulted for the recurrent situations and personalities in his books, but it is perhaps his profound knowledge of these imagined lives, deepened in book after book, that has enabled him to construct the sure and beautiful architecture of *The Galton Case* and *The Goodbye Look* and *The Zebra-Striped Hearse*.

Along with their upwardly mobile characters, Ross Macdonald's books moved away from the tough and lowdown world that was the hardboiled novel's traditional domain. To many (although obviously not to Macdonald), there might be something comfortingly genteel about those elite Californians, no matter how degenerate they turned out to be. They lived in a world of dazzling beaches, long satisfying sweeps of lawn, patios where at brunch the best Bloody Marys might be expected. It is a milieu in which the newcomer stands to lose not his teeth or the back of his skull, but merely his soul. Not so often does Lew Archer find himself in the dusty speakeasies and murderous back alleys where the Continental Op was wont to roam. Rat-infested wharves have given way to private marinas, and opium dens to legally prescribed antidepressants, to ease the refined neuroses of an industrialist gentry whose main problem is boredom.

Much energy would be devoted, in the Fifties as in most periods, to the contemplation of such lives. The Cinemascope screen provided the perfect format for showing off the spacious homes of leisured sinners whose wealth could never make up for that spiritual emptiness as the limousine cruised imperially along the mile-long driveway. And if the sins were not too graphic, it would make a good show for the Radio City Music Hall.

The suburbs had arrived. They were not quite the world of *Ten North Frederick* and *From the Terrace*, but it was close enough that people all over America could identify with the adulteries and violations of Grace Metalious' *Peyton Place*. It had to do with where you lived, and although an old Connecticut town stocked with certifiable patricians, breeders of horses (and themselves exemplary specimens of WASP breeding), differed somewhat from the Levittowns that were spreading rapidly around the outskirts of the cities, there was enough common imagery—of lawn and pool and long morning silence interrupted only by the clatter of milk bottles at the front door—to bridge the gap. Suburban narratives would evolve, different in kind from big-city narratives.

But there was a new kind of big-city narrative as well, featuring not a lonely aging heroic figure but rather a whole squadron of the young, uniformed, and terrifying. Gangs and juvenile delinquents were not new phenomena, of course. Legends of Hell's Kitchen and the Gas House Gang went back decades into an already archaic past, while more recently the wayward children of the Depression had been transformed into the Dead End Kids and the Bowery Boys. More disturbingly, an early Thirties film called *Wild Boys of the Road* had depicted young vagrants as potential revolutionaries, waging violent battle against police until the federal government stepped in to bring harmony to the situation. The final scene, where a benign judge tells the repentant delinquents of "the new spirit in this country," while nodding up at a huge photograph of Franklin D. Roosevelt, had the kind of swelling political emotion usually associated with Soviet or Fascist filmmaking. In any case, the delinquents of the Thirties were seen very much as part of the overall situation, younger versions of the adult delinquents personified by Humphrey Bogart and Edward G. Robinson or by the errant heroes of James M. Cain. These were the kids James T. Farrell had written

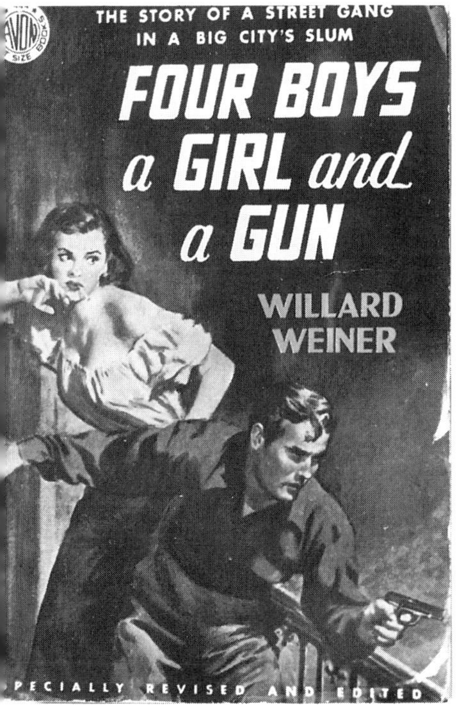

·von 444 (1952)

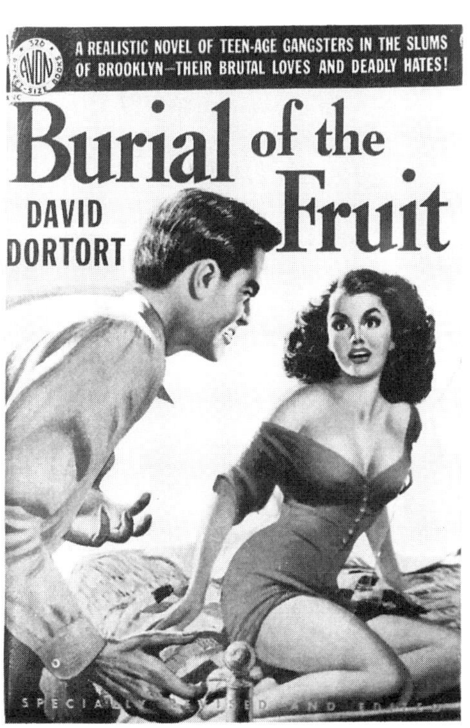

Avon 326 (1951)

ocket Books/Cardinal C-187 (1955)
rtist: Clark Hulings

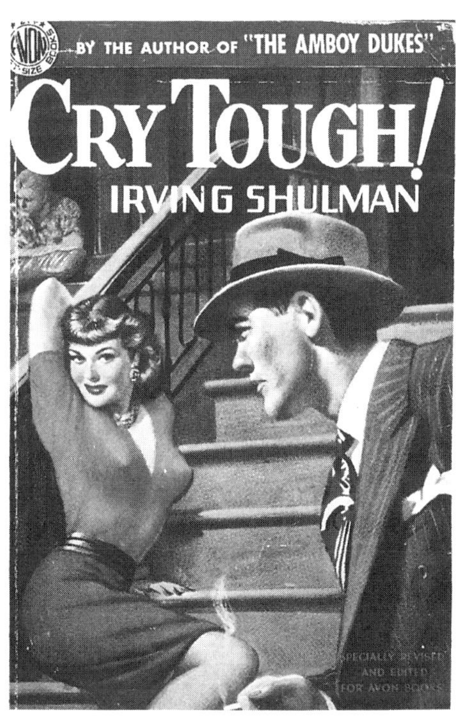

Avon 244 (1950)

about in the *Studs Lonigan* trilogy, ordinary American kids, whose very familiarity made for the persuasiveness of books like Farrell's.

During the War something changed. Behind the flag waving, the home-front unity drummed up by all the media and exemplified in a film like *Since You Went Away*, the teenagers of America were not behaving as expected. Juvenile crime rates soared; gang wars boomed. Magazines were flooded with reports of youthful wrongdoing: *Collier's* asked the question, "Are Children Worse in Wartime?" while *Christian Century* spoke of "Juvenile Delinquency and the War" and *Life* gave ominous coverage to "Boy Gangs of New York: 500 Fighting Units." Even John D. Rockefeller III found time to devote to "Salvaging the Young Criminal."

It was an embarrassment, an affront to morale, and when the war ended it didn't go away. "These kids" were no longer recognizable as facsimiles of one's own youth, so that when Irving Shulman in 1947 published *The Amboy Dukes*, the response was not recognition but horror, and a condemnation directed not only against the characters in the book but against Shulman as well. Five years afterwards, testimony was presented before the Gathings Committee to the effect that *The Amboy Dukes* could be held partly responsible for the tremendous upsurge in juvenile crime in the postwar years. But it was no use putting the blame on Shulman alone; he was soon joined by a whole generation of novelists taking youth crime as their theme.

There were—among many others—Willard Motley (*Knock On Any Door*), David Dortort (*Burial of the Fruit*), Hal Ellson (*Tomboy*), Evan Hunter (*The Blackboard Jungle*), Harlan Ellison (*Rumble*), Wenzell Brown (*Gang Girl*), Morton Cooper (*Delinquent!*), Albert L. Quandt (*Zip-Gun Angels*), writing books often filled with moral indignation and even some perceptive analysis, but also with enough raw realism to satisfy the prurience of their readers, of whom there were many. *Amboy Dukes* sold nearly 4 million copies, and *Blackboard Jungle* went on to become an enormously successful M-G-M movie, having already earned the title of Most Thumbed Paperback by reason of its celebrated attempted-rape scene.

It was a curious phenomenon that seemed to creep out from under the prevailing genres of the day, creating its own audience as it went along. The juvenile-delinquency novel had one great advantage in that it could effortlessly be all things to all people: social tract directed against hoodlums, social tract directed against society, modern cowboy story, pornographic novel in which all the sex could be justified in the name of naturalism, and finally a subversive hymn of praise to the delinquents themselves, to be enjoyed by the same audience that flocked to see Marlon Brando in *The Wild One* in 1951.

It was a perfect opportunity to play the game of redeeming social content, so that Avon Books, in its 1951 edition of *Burial of the Fruit*, could feature a cover painting of an impossibly busty, nearly naked beauty who seems to have just emerged from the nearest hairdressing salon, backing away from one of Avon's usual wooden-featured males with clenched fingers, while the inside jacket copy told how "*Burial of the Fruit* 'hammers home' an understanding of how poor environment, lack of parental control, and absence of properly supervised recreation warp the lives of our children. The book should be read by mothers, fathers, and civil authorities—for *they* are the ones who *can* and *must* eliminate the causes of real life tragedies such as that of Honey Halpern!"

There was something about juvenile delinquents that broke down the already minimal inhibitions of the paperback copywriters. For a whole decade a select list of adjectives was run into the ground: "brutal," "shocking," "frightening," "frank," "vicious," "searing." The effort to go beyond that handful of words elicited fragments of prose that were themselves rather searing:

> Her combat uniform was blue jeans, her vicious weapon a beer-can opener . . . Why do they go wrong? It's a frightening answer—as frightening as the living nightmare of the violence-crazed teen-age cult portrayed in *The Young Punks*. (*The Young Punks*, Pyramid, 1957)

> It started at a wild beach party—with emotions rising to a fever as the bonfire leaped in the darkness, and the hot jazz pounded out of the phonograph . . . And it ended in the cold, early hours of the morning when mayhem and robbery led to STARK VIOLENCE—and TRAGEDY! (*Juvenile Jungle*, Avon, 1957)

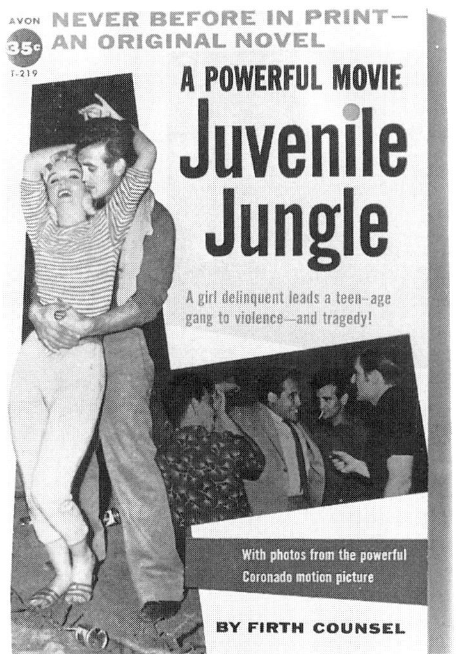

Avon T-219 (1957)

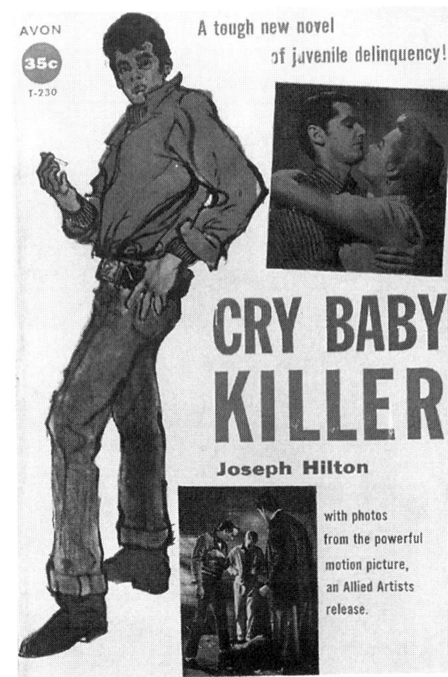

Avon T-230 (1957)

> . . . a jagged gash of reality cut from the living terror of J.D. A startling story of that 3% of our youth, without decent direction in life, running riot with the dark, dangerous impulses of a rock 'n' roll, jet-propelled age. (*Cry Baby Killer*, Avon, 1958)

It was all just *too much*, the phenomenon they were attempting breathlessly and half-incoherently to verbalize. Somehow the heart of it eluded them, no matter how many high-powered adjectives were poured on, no matter how many concerted efforts were made to hit the book buyer over the head. "These kids" had taken on a life of their own. The writers were not shaping them; they were being shaped by them. The kids had entered another realm, were now mythological creatures exercising a power that no sociological analysis could cope with.

That fusion of the demonic and the erotic was sending out perceptible waves, and America palpitated a little with the shock of it. It was far more potent than some downbeat naturalistic study—in the tradition

Bantam F3067 (1957)

of Dreiser, Stephen Crane, and James T. Farrell—of underprivileged kids, spiritual poverty, an unfulfilling environment of decaying alleyways and leaky roofs. Those actual gray lives had been magically transformed into glamorous pulsating ritual presences, presences that seemed effortlessly to capture the stray energies of the society. They radiated sex, fear, and power, amid trancelike patterns of rhythm and group formations. Fetishism had gone wild. Hal Ellson's *Tomboy* was a reasonably serious account of girl gangs, but the girl that James Bama painted for one Bantam edition was no pitiable underprivileged kid but an outrageous manifestation of kinky energy, whose blonde ponytail, leather jacket, and tight blue jeans raised her to the top ranks of erotic iconography, an image that will be remembered long after the text is forgotten.

But in general the paperbacks were outclassed this time. There was no way they could do more than trot along behind the movies, the music, the television images, trying none too imaginatively to capture some of the magic for their own profit. The best cover art in the world could not compete with a few bars of "Jailhouse Rock" or "High School Confidential," and it had long since been demonstrated that a photograph of James Dean was worth a thousand oil paintings.

It was the shiver of the new. New forms were springing up on all sides, and making those carefully composed Signet covers, for instance, seem already stuffy, a rapidly fading memory of an era suddenly extinct. Strange gods had materialized where least expected. They were not of the same breed of people, these new ones. Rumors of outlandish tongues, arcane rites, alien belief systems—alien emotions even—spread naturally in the wake of the sightings. And there would be others, too, of course, not teenagers but adults of a new variety, "restless, jaded men and women, with no aim in life except a new sensation—drugs, 'way-out' jazz, perverted sex, actual crime," as the blurb for Albert Zugsmith's novel *The Beat Generation* would have it.

An imminent explosion was just under the surface, readying itself to shatter the orderly frames, rooms, houses. There would be vented an accumulated disgust stored up behind social forms that had atrophied, forms that had not quite been able to come to grips with a world sud-

Avon 424 (1952)

denly more dangerous. New spaces were opening, and familiar things, old things, could begin to seem grotesque.

The paperback covers of that time repeatedly show a man staring at a woman whose glance is turned away from him. His expression is probably meant to denote lust, but in its sullen intensity it could equally denote fear, suspicion, shame, rage. The only thing not in doubt is the object of his glance. As for the woman, her expression is even more indecipherable. Is it desire? Flirtation? Hatred? Boredom? Her glance goes off into space. She could be thinking of anything or nothing, while he plainly can be thinking of only one thing. It is a strange lull—no action, nothing but thoughts filling the tawdry room—a picture of an emotional void.

What is conveyed, finally, is a sense of ponderousness—as if the bodies of these people were made of concrete, of lead, and their emotions were leaden as well. There is nothing mercurial here, nothing that leaps, nothing elliptical, but rather a slow heavy ache, each individual a monolithic chunk of feeling hopelessly separated from the others. People drag their bodies around like objects they are shackled to, among all the other objects of which their world is made up. The eternal blonde of the paperback covers is a granite weight, a harsh embodiment of a desire that is one of the three or four simple signals beeping out night and day, relentlessly, like a demented telegraph.

The place—America in, say, 1955—is awash in sullen emotions that toss listlessly amid the overwhelming physical reality of everything. Desire of every kind is pervasive. But it is clumsy, uncertain of itself, unable to cut itself free from the forbidding entanglements that close in to choke it. Freedom becomes a vision of some etheric Reno, money cascading orgasmically from an enchanted slot machine, mink and baize shimmering under red lights, to the tune of expensive liquor pouring over ice—a delirium. It's all within his grasp, it has never been so near, not in all the centuries of human effort; he can see it just over the line, just beyond the border of his neighborhood—the glitter of fulfillment. A buck, a blonde, a Buick, a steak dinner, bottle after bottle of champagne, a color television—everything and anything that you could hold in your hand, *really* see, *really* touch, before it slips away, the dream ending, and he wakes on his familiar stony pillow, in the confined spaces of his life, consumed with images of the golden kingdom.

He's a citizen, this Everyman, of a materialist society. Religion is Rock Hudson starring in a remake of *The Magnificent Obsession*. Ghosts have been replaced by scientifically mutated insects. Who needs religion when time and space have been conquered (or nearly so) and when science and capitalism working in tandem can promise a future of instant gratification, a toy world, the biggest Christmas present ever? Nobody needs it—that's the answer. Nobody needs anything, except the right amount of cash to open the magic doors. After all, this is the most prosperous nation in the history of the world; we've got it all; we're keeping it.

In Frank Tashlin's 1957 film, *Will Success Spoil Rock Hunter?*, a newly promoted advertising executive (Tony Randall), alone in his office at night, experiences solitary ecstasy as switchboards and typewriters function by themselves, doors swing open in obedience to his will, lights flash, and Jayne Mansfield—clad only in a thin layer of dollar bills—dances around his desk as an invisible choir sings "You've got it made, you've got it made." Heaven, in the Fifties sense, is a room full of the latest in modern design, full of shiny new manufactured objects, all of them belonging to you. It is a dream of safety, of calm lawns, of picture windows flooding new light on what were zones of shadow. A rectangular world of well-ordered limits has almost succeeded in eliminating the unseen and unpalpable. Years later a mournful Peggy Lee song would serve as postmortem on the underlying anxiety of the time: "Is that all there is?"

But something unexpected happens. The pure materialist perception of the world proves to be not so pure. The physical objects themselves—those controlled things—become charged with supernatural energy. The mind makes gods and demons out of the materials at hand. America, the ultimate secular society, could not prevent the inanimate man-made trappings of its life from assuming nightmarish proportions. The dreamer whose heaven is full of things suffers the fate of the fairy-tale character whose wish, too well fulfilled, shatters him. Sex and money, the only objects of desire, lure the individual into places of archaic horror, where monstrous transformations occur. Desire, enraged

Bantam 717 (1945)
Artist: Ken Riley

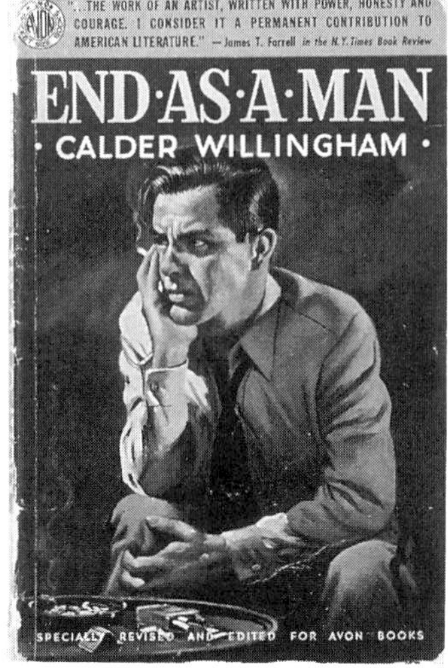

Avon 240 (1950)

that it cannot be fulfilled, that the promise was false, turns desperate, paranoid, violent. It destroys what it cannot possess, what it could never have possessed.

The whole place is shaking with a violent struggle to acquire the objects that bestow happiness. From *The Blackboard Jungle* to *Executive Suite*, all is conflict; and within the family, within the marriages, the conflict renews itself. Some central crack in the great design has unleashed the forces of imbalance. A troubling wobble can be felt, which no appliance, however white or solid, can steady. There is no relief from it, no peace. The nagging itch is always there, demanding action. When it comes, the action is frantic and purposeless, the action of people on the edge trying to stave off an inevitable breakdown.

Consider the man who stares out from the cover of the paperback, his fist clenched, an open bottle beside him, the ashtray before him heaped with cigarettes. His face is rigid with tension. Between his eyes there is a deep vertical crease that seems carved in stone. The mouth is fixed in a grimace; the eyes wince, as if in pain from the pressures his own head exerts against him. The title of this tableau could be "Portrait of a Man Facing a Brick Wall." We may be sure that he will eventually act—and violently—but there will be no conviction behind his act, only the convulsive effort to free himself from this intolerable solitude. "All our misery," wrote Pascal, "comes from not knowing how to be alone in a room." And Chandler's Marlowe, alone in his room: "I looked at my watch. I looked at the wall. I looked at nothing."

So, in a thousand American cities and towns, the same man directs his vacant gaze out office window and motel window, from park bench, from bus and train, across the lawn, down the street, waiting for the thing—what is it?—that will crack the deathly stillness of the suburban afternoon or bring a breath of excitement, a fresh breeze, to the stagnant urban evening. In the meantime, he pours himself another short one, lights up another Camel, and reads, perhaps, a paperback novel as the minutes tick by, perhaps the one (*Border Town Girl*, by John D. MacDonald) that begins: "The tall girl was restless. She had dark eyes with a hard flickering light in them, like black opals. Her mouth was wide and soft and sullen. It was ten o'clock at night in Baker, Texas. Her third-floor room in the Sage House had the hot breathlessness of the bakery she had once worked in—back when she was fourteen and had looked eighteen . . ."

This is the music of his own world, the one he lives in. It has the same air, the same weather, the same floors and walls and cars, the hot evenings, the eyes glimpsed for an instant looking out from someone else's porch. This is no dream; it's the very stuff of reality, as real as the thick paper of the book cover against his fingers. As real as the radio report crackling into the room from another outpost of reality. For sure, it's happening out there, somewhere in the neon wilderness, in the asphalt jungle. A woman screams. The lights go out. A window breaks. There's a siren, a shot, a dark figure running down the street. The shriek of the saxophone through the nightclub's swinging doors, a body slumped over a steering wheel in an empty lot, a telephone ringing for someone who can't answer, the elevator rising ominously toward the penthouse floor. And he's in the middle of it somehow, he's on the ledge, just coming through the door, peering through the latticework, crouching silently in the stairwell as the assassin goes by, his knees poised to spring forward. He reads it as another might read a lyric poem—because its images sustain the life in him.

Epilogue

The Long Morning After

When he awoke the saxophone was not a saxophone anymore, although the approximation was uncannily precise. Likewise the shattering glass, the howl of the squad car, the old-style telephone ringing in the empty suite. All had been sampled, while he slept, and their places taken by digitalized replicas which could be played back an infinite number of times without visible degradation (the noise filtered through a NoNoise system). Ideally they were to be not merely played back but recombined to generate a thousand alternate narratives, with personalized music tracks available upon application.

None of the elements had gone away. Each piece remembered distinctly from the former time had been absorbed into a repertoire permanently hungry for usable ingredients. There was no telling when a particular detail might be needed: the snap of a garter belt, the sheen of a leather holster, the background harmonies of an ancient radio jingle, the sudden grating incursion of a wisecrack uttered by a gum-chewing waitress.

There were electronic maws to be fed. The pop culture of the recent past was a fossil fuel deposit which the thing that called itself multimedia could suck almost indefinitely into its pipelines, providing energy for the ten thousand channels which could not run without something or other filling their screens, some chase, some threat, some glimpse of transparent lace, at the very least some hairdo or snatch of tune.

That time recently passed had done some considerable damage to the notion of orderly progression. Things now moved backward just as easily as forward, or sideways into unanticipated gulches, apt for ambush. It had been, not so long ago, the era when the faces of missing children appeared on milk cartons to haunt the breakfasts of America. Was that before or after the era when secret rings of Satanic abusers started to emerge from the testimony of children flanked by court-appointed therapists and small-town police chiefs, or when heavily-armed religious spokesmen began laying down the blueprints for future confrontations with Federal marshals, or when ritual scarification became a matter of fashion, or when a man could be plucked from obscurity into a full-fledged media career on the strength of having his penis severed by his wife, or when strong evidence for alien abduction began to be introduced into the conversation of Ivy League professors? The soundtrack had been readied some years earlier: was that Talking Heads' "Psycho Killer" or Unnatural Axe's "They Saved Hitler's Brain" providing an elegant homage to white noise in the background? The reverb pretty much drowned out the chatter of the children on the corner—the ones not yet abducted by Satanists or aliens—as they traded their serial killer cards, a Dahmer for a Bundy, two Specks for a Manson.

Hence the eternal return of *Detour* and *Gun Crazy*. The circular for the new dance club was adorned with James Avati's cover painting for the Signet paperback of Horace McCoy's *Kiss Tomorrow Goodbye*, and inside the club they were projecting Betty Page bondage loops resurrected from some lost basement of Eisenhower's America. It all managed to convey a nostalgia for what had never quite happened but might possibly be about to happen, a mix-and-match collage of hot-button fetish items (mail-ordered from Frederick's of Hollywood before their stock was looted in the L.A. riots) juxtaposed with lobby cards of movie melodramas about homicidally jealous housewives, compliant strippers, and delivery men drawn haplessly into elaborate but doomed heists. The clothes were appropriately retro, and so was the music: the road from punk had by now detoured into music retrieved from the same cocktail lounge where Robert Mitchum danced with Jean Simmons in *Angel Face*, bongo exotica piped directly into the hotel room where the traveling salesman is planning how to complete his con job on the divorcee across the hall.

He woke up vaguely remembering a movie so new it hadn't been released yet: Miramax presents Chow Yun-fat and Alanis Morissette co-starring in an adaptation of an unpublished Jim Thompson novella incorporating lost out-takes from Ed Wood porno movies, with special guest appearances by Mamie Van Doren, Barbara Steele, and Joe Don Baker, and soundtrack adapted by John Zorn from newly remastered unreleased tapes by Arthur Lyman (the legendary "Que Viva Carioca" sessions). The only thing he really remembered from it was the stripper whispering, "The past doesn't stand still, it changes just like everything else in this crazy world."

By 1993 Dell had announced that its new paperback line Edge would feature "noir mysteries in the vein of Jim Thompson." For Jim Thompson to end up as a brand name capped a process that had included the republication of most of his significant writings (with Barry Gifford's Black Lizard imprint leading the way), the filming of a cluster of his novels and the optioning of many more, and the inclusion of a Thompson adaptation in the slickly produced cable television series *Fallen Angels*, which also drew on the work of Raymond Chandler and James Ellroy. Having nearly exhausted the repackaging potential of Thompson's own work, it stood to reason that the next step would be the production of up-to-date ersatz Thompson to satisfy the newly created market.

It was a tribute to Thompson's singularity that after so many decades his writing could still function as a symbol of the "edge," as if the author of *The Nothing Man* had defined for all time a zero degree not just of writing but of being. In some ways he appeared to inhabit a zone beyond nostalgia. Yet the implausible chic which made his name the convenient symbol for a highly profitable nihilism—an aura perfectly compatible with grunge, body-piercing, and other accessories of cultural fashion—could not help but evoke an ironic contrast with the world that Thompson had inhabited.

What would once have been inconceivable was that Jim Thompson should seem, if not exactly a voice of reason, then at least a reassuring voice from down home, a both-feet-on-the-ground messenger from a time and place where things looked just as cheap as they were. In the faux-Roman atriums of the mega-malls, amid the shrink-wrapped luxuries of microchip art, any reminder of the drab and sullen world of Thompson's bellhops and roughnecks carried the pungent force of real blood, real oil stains.

On one level Thompson's writing had come to be valued for its radical unpalatability, the violent instability of its quarrel with the world, all the qualities that made Thompson in his own time a marginal writer at best. The borderline viability of his books, when they first came out in the 50s, had come from their passing resemblance to the more satisfyingly orchestrated popular fiction of Harry Whittington or Day Keene. Nonetheless those books, like so many of the old paperbacks, had begun to seem remnants of an American culture now shredded past recognition, emblems of a vanished authenticity.

But did that authenticity belong to Thompson—or, in their different ways, David Goodis or Horace McCoy or Day Keene himself—or to the world of which they wrote? If Thompson was supremely alienated, there had at least been a world for him to be alienated from. His industrial wastelands and hellish hotel rooms, his bus stations steeped in boredom and simmering disgust, represented some kind of geography, some minimal sense of location. He may have evoked it only to destroy it, but it had after all been there for him to destroy. His books spoke of a time when it was still unusual to feel the way his heroes felt, or at least to acknowledge the fact. It had become in retrospect a heroic period: gratuitous evil and affectless violence *meant* something back then. There was still enough sense of self to register the self's erosion.

Not that conditions had not always been comparably chaotic. A book like Luc Sante's mythic documentary *Low Life* (1991), with its infernal vision of the criminal underworld of 19th-century New York, easily matched the tabloid horrors currently retailed by the true crime industry. The only difference lay in the style, the packaging: what had been marginal was now mainstream. The aberrant, no longer having any standard against which to measure itself, attained a baroque phase of self-conscious embellishment.

The elements once consigned to a cultural underworld of paperback novels and drive-in movies and jukebox music—the world of *Police Gazette* and *True Confessions*, of semi-legal sex movies and fetish comics—now dominated the niches abandoned by Doris Day and Edward R. Murrow. Stephen King had long since replaced Allen Drury and Arthur Hailey Jr., just as *The Silence of the Lambs* had replaced *Ben Hur*, and "infotainment" reenactments of drug busts had replaced news analyses of social and political policy. The long suburban Sunday afternoon was devoted to made-for-TV movies about incest, rape, and domestic murder. In such a context it was difficult to imagine a netherworld not already on full display.

But that there was such a netherworld—and that in due course it would make itself visible in ways wholly novel, and no doubt wholly unacceptable—was hardly to be doubted. Surely even the unconscious has an unconscious, an unconscious which may choose temporarily to disguise itself in a discarded mask. "The past doesn't really stand still . . ."

The whisper stopped short and he found himself gazing once again at the old cover tacked to the wall. The figures depicted in it—the blonde staring at the discolored ceiling, the washed-up con man coaxing a last puff out of his remnant of cigarette, the other woman poised in the doorway looking on in an indecipherable mix of surprise and contempt—seemed awkwardly frozen, as if they had been caught out in some furtive movement he had not been meant to discern.

Appendix

The Hardboiled Era: A Checklist, 1929–1960

The following list is designed to show the hardboiled novel not as a series of isolated literary works but as part of an ongoing cycle, virtually an industrial phenomenon. Most of the writers worked fast in a highly competitive and innovative area, where each decisive success had its effects on the books that came afterwards. Spinoffs, copies, fusions abounded.

Since contrasts are more interesting than rigidly defined categories, I have thrown into the mix a variety of dissimilar works, naturalistic novels, political novels, spy thrillers, conventional whodunits: all those books that seem to orbit near the undefinable quantity I have referred to as the hardboiled novel. The reader can create his own system of pigeonholes. My purpose has been simply to locate the books in their chronological landscape so that new relationships among them can be perceived.

Dates are usually those of first publication in book form. Exceptions include James Cain's *Double Indemnity*, which did not appear in hardcover until seven years after its magazine serialization, and Horace McCoy's *Corruption City*, a movie treatment which was published posthumously as a novel six years after it was written. Many of these books have traveled under various titles, and I cannot claim to have recorded every variant.

1929
W.R. Burnett: *Little Caesar*
Carroll John Daly: *The Hidden Hand*
Dashiell Hammett: *Red Harvest, The Glass Key*
Ellery Queen: *The Roman Hat Mystery*
S.S. Van Dine: *The Bishop Murder Case*

1930
W.R. Burnett: *Iron Man*
James M. Cain: *Our Government*
Donald Henderson Clarke: *Louis Beretti*
Carroll John Daly: *The Tag Murders*
Dashiell Hammett: *The Maltese Falcon*
Raoul Whitfield: *Green Ice*

1931
Carroll John Daly: *Tainted Power, The Third Murderer*
William Faulkner: *Sanctuary*
Dashiell Hammett: *The Glass Key*
Raoul Whitfield: *Death in a Bowl, Danger Zone*

1932
Paul Cain: *Fast One*
Erskine Caldwell: *Tobacco Road*
Raoul Whitfield: *The Virgin Kills*

1933
W.R. Burnett: *Dark Hazard*
Erskine Caldwell: *God's Little Acre*
Carroll John Daly: *The Amateur Murderer, Murder Won't Wait*
Dashiell Hammett: *Woman in the Dark*
Nathanael West: *Miss Lonelyhearts*

1934
James M. Cain: *The Postman Always Rings Twice*
Dashiell Hammett: *The Thin Man*
John O'Hara: *Appointment in Samarra*

1935
Edward Anderson: *Hungry Men*
Carroll John Daly: *Murder from the East*
William Faulkner: *Pylon*
Tom Kroner: *Waiting for Nothing*
Jonathan Latimer: *Murder in the Madhouse*, *Headed for a Hearse*
Horace McCoy: *They Shoot Horses, Don't They?*
John O'Hara: *Butterfield 8*
Don Tracy: *Criss Cross*

1936
James M. Cain: *Double Indemnity*
Carroll John Daly: *Mr. Strang*, *The Mystery of the Smoking Gun*
Graham Greene: *A Gun for Sale* [*This Gun for Hire*]
Jonathan Latimer: *The Lady in the Morgue*
Frederick Nebel: *Fifty Roads to Town*

1937
Edward Anderson: *Thieves Like Us*
James M. Cain: *Serenade*
Donald Henderson Clarke: *Confidential*
Carroll John Daly: *Emperor of Evil*
Ernest Hemingway: *To Have and Have Not*
Horace McCoy: *No Pockets in a Shroud*
Don Tracy: *How Sleeps the Beast*

1938
Dorothy Baker: *Young Man with a Horn*
Robert Leslie Bellem: *Blue Murder*
A.I. Bezzerides: *Long Haul* [*They Drive By Night*]
James M. Cain: *Career in C Major*
James Hadley Chase: *No Orchids for Miss Blandish*
David Goodis: *Retreat from Oblivion*
Richard Hallas [a.k.a. Eric Knight]: *You Play the Black and the Red Comes Up*
Gerald Kersh: *Night and the City*
Jonathan Latimer: *The Dead Don't Care*
Horace McCoy: *I Should Have Stayed Home*
John O'Hara: *Hope of Heaven*
Roger Torrey: *42 Days for Murder*

1939
Eric Ambler: *A Coffin for Dimitrios, Cause for Alarm*
Raymond Chandler: *The Big Sleep*
John Fante: *Ask the Dust*
William Faulkner: *The Wild Palms*
Kenneth Fearing: *The Hospital*
Graham Greene: *Confidential Agent*
Brett Halliday: *Dividend on Death*
Geoffrey Household: *Rogue Male*
Jonathan Latimer: *Red Gardenias*
Nathanael West: *The Day of the Locust*

1940
Cleve Adams: *Sabotage*
Eric Ambler: *Journey into Fear*
W.R. Burnett: *High Sierra*
James M. Cain: *The Embezzler*
Raymond Chandler: *Farewell, My Lovely*
Frank Gruber: *The French Key, The Laughing Fox*
Dorothy B. Hughes: *The So Blue Marble, The Cross-Eyed Bear Murders*
Jonathan Latimer: *Dark Memory*
John O'Hara: *Pal Joey*
James Ross: *They Don't Dance Much*
Percival Wilde: *Inquest*
Cornell Woolrich: *The Bride Wore Black*

1941
Nelson Algren: *Never Come Morning*
James M. Cain: *Mildred Pierce*
Kenneth Fearing: *Dagger of the Mind* [*Cry Murder!*]
Steve Fisher: *I Wake Up Screaming*
Jonathan Latimer: *Solomon's Vineyard* [*The Fifth Grave*]
Maritta Wolf: *Whistle Stop*
Cornell Woolrich: *The Black Curtain*

1942
James M. Cain: *Love's Lovely Counterfeit*
Raymond Chandler: *The High Window*
Kenneth Fearing: *Clark Gifford's Body*
James Gunn: *Deadlier Than the Male*
Dorothy B. Hughes: *The Fallen Sparrow*
Ellery Queen: *Calamity Town*

Richard Sale: *Lazarus #7, Passing Strange*
Jim Thompson: *Now and On Earth*
Cornell Woolrich: *Phantom Lady, Black Alibi*

1943
Vera Caspary: *Laura*
Raymond Chandler: *The Lady in the Lake*
Graham Greene: *The Ministry of Fear*
Dorothy B. Hughes: *The Blackbirder*
Margaret Millar: *Wall of Eyes*
Ira Wolfert: *Tucker's People*
Cornell Woolrich: *The Black Angel*

1944
W.R. Burnett: *Nobody Lives Forever*
Samuel Fuller: *The Dark Page*
Dorothy B. Hughes: *The Delicate Ape, Johnnie*
Ross Macdonald: *The Dark Tunnel*
Cornell Woolrich: *The Black Path of Fear, Deadline at Dawn*

1945
Brett Halliday: *Murder Is My Business*
Dorothy B. Hughes: *Dread Journey*
Joel Townsley Rogers: *The Red Right Hand*
Leonard Q. Ross [Leo C. Rosten]: *The Dark Corner*
Cornell Woolrich: *Night Has a Thousand Eyes*

1946
James M. Cain: *Past All Dishonor*
Helen Eustis: *The Horizontal Man*
John Evans: *Halo in Blood*
Kenneth Fearing: *The Big Clock*
David Goodis: *Dark Passage*
William Lindsay Gresham: *Nightmare Alley*
Chester Himes: *If He Hollers Let Him Go*
Geoffrey Homes [Daniel Mainwaring]: *Build My Gallows High*
Roy Huggins: *The Double Take*
Dorothy B. Hughes: *Ride the Pink Horse*
Ross Macdonald: *Trouble Follows Me*
Wade Miller: *Deadly Weapon*
Richard Sale: *Benefit Performance*
Jim Thompson: *Heed the Thunder*

1947
Nelson Algren: *The Neon Wilderness*
Robert Bloch: *The Scarf*
Fredric Brown: *The Fabulous Clipjoint*
James M. Cain: *The Butterfly*, *Sinful Woman*
Jay Dratler: *The Pitfall*
John Evans: *If You Have Tears*
David Goodis: *Nightfall*, *Behold This Woman*
Chester Himes: *Lonely Crusade*
Roy Huggins: *Too Late for Tears*
Dorothy B. Hughes: *In a Lonely Place*
Howard Hunt: *Stranger in Town*
Eleazer Lipsky: *Kiss of Death*
Ross Macdonald: *Blue City*
Wade Miller: *Guilty Bystander*
Willard Motley: *Knock on Any Door*
Irving Shulman: *The Amboy Dukes*
Mickey Spillane: *I, the Jury*
Cornell Woolrich: *Waltz into Darkness*

1948
Fredric Brown: *Dead Ringer*, *Murder Can Be Fun*
James M. Cain: *The Moth*
John Evans: *Halo for Satan*
Howard Hunt: *Maelstrom*
Ross Macdonald: *The Three Roads*
Horace McCoy: *Kiss Tomorrow Goodbye*
Wade Miller: *Uneasy Street*
Cornell Woolrich: *Rendezvous in Black*, *I Married a Dead Man*

1949
Nelson Algren: *The Man with the Golden Arm*
A.I. Bezzerides: *Thieves' Market*
Fredric Brown: *The Screaming Mimi*, *The Bloody Moonlight*
W.R. Burnett: *The Asphalt Jungle*
Raymond Chandler: *The Little Sister*
Hal Ellson: *Duke*
John Evans: *Halo in Brass*
Graham Greene: *The Third Man*
Patricia Highsmith: *Strangers on a Train*
Roy Huggins: *Lovely Lady, Pity Me*
Dorothy B. Hughes: *The Big Barbecue*

Howard Hunt: *Bimini Run*
William Krasner: *Walk the Dark Streets*
Ross Macdonald: *The Moving Target*
Jim Thompson: *Nothing More Than Murder*

1950
Bill Ballinger: *Portrait in Smoke*
Robert Leslie Bellem: *The Window with the Sleeping Nude*
Fredric Brown: *Night of the Jabberwock*, *Compliments of a Fiend*, *Here Comes a Candle*
James M. Cain: *Jealous Woman*
Hal Ellson: *Tomboy*
David Goodis: *Of Missing Persons*
Dorothy B. Hughes: *The Candy Kid*
Eleazer Lipsky: *The People Against O'Hara*
John D. MacDonald: *The Brass Cupcake*
Ross Macdonald: *The Drowning Pool*
William P. McGivern: *Very Cold for May*
Mickey Spillane: *My Gun Is Quick*, *Vengeance Is Mine*
Harry Whittington: *Slay Ride for a Lady*
Cornell Woolrich: *Savage Bride*

1951
Gil Brewer: *13 French Street*
Fredric Brown: *The Far Cry*, *Death Has Many Doors*
Kenneth Fearing: *The Loneliest Girl in the World*
David Goodis: *Cassidy's Girl*
Day Keene: *To Kiss or Kill*, *Farewell to Passion* [*The Passion Murders*]
John D. MacDonald: *Murder for the Bride*, *Judge Me Not*, *Weep for Me*
Ross Macdonald: *The Way Some People Die*
William P. McGivern: *Shield for Murder*
Mickey Spillane: *One Lonely Night*, *The Big Kill*, *The Long Wait*
Harry Whittington: *Fires That Destroy*, *Married to Murder*
Charles Williams: *Hill Girl*, *Big City Girl*, *River Girl*
Cornell Woolrich: *Strangler's Serenade*

1952
Fredric Brown: *The Deep End*, *We All Killed Grandma*
David Goodis: *Of Tender Sin*, *Street of the Lost*
Chester Himes: *Cast the First Stone*
Dorothy B. Hughes: *The Davidian Report*
David Karp: *The Brotherhood of Velvet*

John D. MacDonald: *The Damned*
Ross Macdonald: *The Ivory Grin*
Horace McCoy: *Scalpel, Corruption City* [published 1959]
William P. McGivern: *The Big Heat, The Crooked Frame*
Mickey Spillane: *Kiss Me Deadly*
Jim Thompson: *The Killer Inside Me, Cropper's Cabin*
Gore Vidal: *Death in the Fifth Position*
Hilary Waugh: *Last Seen Wearing...*

1953
Fredric Brown: *Madball*
Howard Browne: *Thin Air*
William Burroughs: *Junkie*
James M. Cain: *Galatea*
Raymond Chandler: *The Long Goodbye*
Charles Einstein: *The Bloody Spur*
Ian Fleming: *Casino Royale*
David Goodis: *The Burglar, The Moon in the Gutter*
Davis Grubb: *The Night of the Hunter*
David Karp: *Hardman*
Ira Levin: *A Kiss Before Dying*
John D. MacDonald: *Dead Low Tide, The Neon Jungle, Cancel All Our Vows*
Ross Macdonald: *Meet Me at the Morgue*
Richard Matheson: *Someone Is Bleeding*
Helen Nielsen: *Detour*
Jim Thompson: *Bad Boy, The Alcoholics, Savage Night, Recoil*
Harry Whittington: *So Dead My Love!, Vengeful Sinner* [*Die, Lover*], *Prime Sucker, Sinner's Club, Girl on Parole*
Charles Willeford: *High Priest of California, Wild Wives*
Charles Williams: *Hell Hath No Fury, Nothing in Her Way*

1954
Robert Bloch: *The Kidnapper*
Gil Brewer: *A Killer Is Loose*
Chandler Brossard: *All Passion Spent*
Fredric Brown: *His Name Was Death*
R.V. Cassill: *Dormitory Women*
Steve Fisher: *Giveaway*
David Goodis: *Black Friday, Street of No Return, The Blonde on the Street Corner*
Kenneth Fearing: *The Generous Heart*
William Gwinn: *Jazz Bum*

Patricia Highsmith: *The Blunderer*
Evan Hunter: *The Blackboard Jungle*
Day Keene: *Sleep with the Devil, Notorious, Homicidal Lady*
John D. MacDonald: *Area of Suspicion, All These Condemned, Contrary Pleasure*
Ross Macdonald: *Find a Victim*
William P. McGivern: *Rogue Cop*
George Milburn: *Hoboes and Harlots*
Jim Thompson: *The Golden Gizmo, A Hell of a Woman, The Nothing Man, Roughneck, A Swell-Looking Babe, The Criminal*
Lionel White: *Clean Break* [*The Killing*]
Harry Whittington: *You'll Die Next!, The Woman Is Mine, Saddle the Storm, Wild Oats*
Charles Williams: *Go Home, Stranger, A Touch of Death*

1955
Bill Ballinger: *The Tooth and the Nail*
Fredric Brown: *The Wench Is Dead*
Jay Dratler: *The Judas Kiss*
David Goodis: *The Wounded and the Slain*
W.L. Heath: *Violent Saturday*
Patricia Highsmith: *The Talented Mr. Ripley*
Chester Himes: *The Primitive* [*The End of a Primitive*]
Day Keene: *Who Has Wilma Lathrop?*
Jonathan Latimer: *Sinners and Shrouds*
John D. MacDonald: *A Bullet for Cinderella, Cry Hard, Cry Fast*
Ross Macdonald: *The Name Is Archer*
Margaret Millar: *Beast in View*
Peter Rabe: *Stop This Man, Benny Muscles In, A Shroud for Jesso*
Jim Thompson: *After Dark, My Sweet*
Harry Whittington: *One Got Away*
Charles Willeford: *Pick-Up*
Charles Williams: *Scorpion Reef* [*Gulf Coast Girl*]

1956
Nelson Algren: *A Walk on the Wild Side*
Fredric Brown: *The Lenient Beast*
David Goodis: *Down There* [*Shoot the Piano Player*]
Chester Himes: *The Third Generation*
Day Keene: *Murder on the Side, Bring Him Back Dead*
John D. MacDonald: *Murder in the Wind, April Evil, You Live Once*
Ross Macdonald: *The Barbarous Coast*

Ed McBain: *Cop Hater*, *The Mugger*, *The Pusher*
Whit Masterson: *Badge of Evil* [*Touch of Evil*]
George Milburn: *Julie* [*Old John's Woman*]
Peter Rabe: *A House in Naples*, *Kill the Boss Good-bye*, *Dig My Grave Deep*
Harry Whittington: *Brute in Brass*, *The Humming Box*, *Saturday Night Town*, *Desire in the Dust*
Charles Williams: *The Big Bite*, *The Diamond Bikini*

1957
Bill Ballinger: *The Longest Second*
Ann Bannon: *Odd Girl Out*
Leigh Brackett: *The Tiger Among Us*
David Goodis: *Fire in the Flesh*
W.L. Heath: *Ill Wind*
Patricia Highsmith: *Deep Water*
Chester Himes: *For Love of Imabelle* [*A Rage in Harlem*]
John D. MacDonald: *The Price of Murder*, *Death Trap*, *The Empty Trap*, *A Man of Affairs*
Margaret Millar: *An Air That Kills* [*The Soft Talkers*]
Peter Rabe: *The Out Is Death*, *Agreement to Kill*, *It's My Funeral*, *Journey into Terror*
Jim Thompson: *The Kill-Off*
Harry Whittington: *Temptations of Valerie*, *Man in the Shadow*
Charles Williams: *Girl Out Back*

1958
Fredric Brown: *One for the Road*, *The Office*
Raymond Chandler: *Playback*
Stanley Ellin: *The Eighth Circle*
Patricia Highsmith: *A Game for the Living*
Roy Huggins: *77 Sunset Strip*
Jack Kerouac: *The Subterraneans*
John D. MacDonald: *The Executioners*, *Clemmie*, *Soft Touch*
Ross Macdonald: *The Doomsters*
Ed McBain: *King's Ransom*
Richard Matheson: *A Stir of Echoes*
Peter Rabe: *Mission for Vengeance*, *Blood on the Desert*, *Bring Me Another Corpse*
Jim Thompson: *The Getaway*, *Wild Town*
Harry Whittington: *Web of Murder*
Charles Willeford: *Honey Gal* [*The Black Mass of Brother Springer*]
Charles Williams: *Man on the Run*, *All the Way*

1959
Robert Bloch: *Psycho*
Fredric Brown: *Knock Three-One-Two*, *The Late Lamented*
Richard Condon: *The Manchurian Candidate*
Chester Himes: *The Real Cool Killers*, *The Crazy Kill*
Day Keene: *Take a Step to Murder*, *Too Hot to Hold*
Jonathan Latimer: *Black Is the Fashion for Dying*
Ross Macdonald: *The Galton Case*
Ed McBain: *Killer's Wedge*, *Til Death*
Margaret Millar: *The Listening Walls*
Peter Rabe: *Time Enough to Die*
Harry Whittington: *A Ticket to Hell*, *Halfway to Hell*, *Backwoods Tramp*
Cornell Woolrich: *Death Is My Dancing Partner*

1960
Clarence Cooper, Jr.: *The Scene*
Kenneth Fearing: *The Crozart Story*
Donald Hamilton: *Death of a Citizen*, *The Wrecking Crew*
Patricia Highsmith: *This Sweet Sickness*
Chester Himes: *All Shot Up*, *The Big Gold Dream*
John D. MacDonald: *Slam the Big Door*, *The End of the Night*
Ross Macdonald: *The Ferguson Affair*
Ed McBain: *The Heckler*, *Give the Boys a Great Big Hand*, *See Them Die*
Margaret Millar: *A Stranger in My Grave*
Donald Westlake: *The Mercenaries*
Harry Whittington: *The Devil Wears Wings*, *Hell Can Wait*, *Heat of Night*, *A Night for Screaming*, *Nita's Place*
Charles Willeford: *The Woman Chaser*
John A. Williams: *The Angry Ones* [*One for New York*]
Cornell Woolrich: *The Doom Stone*

Selected Bibliography

Alloway, Lawrence. *Violent America: The Movies, 1946-1964.* New York: The Museum of Modern Art, 1971.

Barnes, Melvyn. *Best Detective Fiction.* Hamden, Conn.: Linnet Books, 1975.

Barson, Michael S. "Fires That Create: The Versatility and Craft of Harry Whittington." *Paperback Quarterly*, vol. IV, no. 2 (Brownwood, Texas: Summer 1981).

Bonn, Thomas L. *Heavy Traffic and High Culture: New American Library as Literary Gatekeeper in the Paperback Revolution.* Carbondale, Ill.: Southern Illinois University Press, 1989.

Bonn, Thomas L. *Undercover: An Illustrated History of American Mass Market Paperbacks.* New York: Penguin, 1982.

Davis, Kenneth C. *Two-Bit Culture: The Paperbacking of America.* Boston: Houghton Mifflin, 1982.

Durham, Philip. *Down These Mean Streets a Man Must Go: Raymond Chandler's Knight.* Chapel Hill, N.C.: University of North Carolina Press, 1963.

Fabbri, Marina and Elisa Resegotti, eds. *I Colori del Nero: Cinema Litteratura Noir.* Milan: Ubulibri, 1989.

Gardiner, Dorothy, & Katherine Sorley Walker, eds. *Raymond Chandler Speaking.* Boston: Houghton Mifflin, 1962.

Garnier, Philippe. *Goodis: La Vie en Noir et Blanc.* Paris, Editions du Seuil, 1984.

Garnier, Philippe. *Honni Soit Qui Malibu: Quelques Ecrivains a Hollywood.* Paris: Bernard Grasset, 1996.

Goodstone, Tony. *The Pulps: Fifty Years of American Pop Culture.* New York: Chelsea House, 1970.

Gordon, Michael. *Juvenile Delinquency in the American Novel, 1905-1965.* New York: Bowling Green University Popular Press, 1971.

Goulart, Ron, ed. *The Hardboiled Dicks: An Anthology of Pulp Detective Fiction*. Los Angeles: Sherbourne Press, 1965.

Guerif, Francois, ed. "Dossier Jim Thompson," *Polar* no. 2 (Paris: May 1979).

Hancer, Kevin. *The Paperback Price Guide*. Cleveland: Overstreet Publications, Inc., 1980.

Hancer, Kevin. *The Paperback Price Guide #2*. New York: Harmony Books, 1982.

Haycraft, Howard, ed. *The Art of the Mystery Story*. New York: Grosset & Dunlap, 1940.

Hellman, Lillian. *An Unfinished Woman*. New York: Little, Brown & Company, 1969.

Hoopes, Roy. *Cain: A Biography of James M. Cain*. New York: Holt, Rinehart, and Winston, 1982.

Johnson, Diane. *Dashiell Hammett: A Life*. New York: Random House, 1983.

Kaplan, Barry Jay. *Love Was Cheap and Life Was High: Postcards from Paperback Cover Art of the 40s and 50s*. New York: Collier Books, 1990.

Landrum, Larry N., Pat Browne and Ray B. Browne, eds. *Dimensions of Detective Fiction*. New York: Popular Press, 1976.

Layman, Richard. *Dashiell Hammett: A Descriptive Bibliography*. Pittsburgh, Pa.: University of Pittsburgh Press, 1979.

Layman, Richard. *Shadow Man: The Life of Dashiell Hammett*. New York: Harcourt Brace Jovanovich, 1981.

Lyles, William H. *Putting Dell on the Map: A History of the Dell Paperbacks*. Greenwood Press, 1984.

Macdonald, Ross. *On Crime Writing*. Capra Press, 1973.

MacShane, Frank. *The Life of Raymond Chandler*. New York: E. P. Dutton, 1976.

MacShane, Frank, ed. *Selected Letters of Raymond Chandler*. New York: Columbia University Press, 1981.

Madden, David, ed. *Tough Guy Writers of the Thirties*. Bloomington, Ill.: Southern Illinois University Press, 1968.

Madden, David. *James M. Cain*. Twayne, 1970.

Neuberg, Victor. *Popular Literature: A History and Guide*. New York: Penguin, 1977.

Nevins, Francis M., Jr. *Cornell Woolrich: First You Dream, Then You Die*. New York: The Mysterious Press, 1988.

Nolan, William F. *Dashiell Hammett: A Casebook*. McNally & Loftin, 1969.

Nolan, William F., ed. *The Black Mask Boys: Masters in the Hard-Boiled School of Detective Fiction*. New York: William Morrow, 1985.

Peterson, Clarence. *The Bantam Story: Thirty Years of Paperback Publishing*, 2nd ed. New York: Bantam Books, 1975.

Polito, Robert. *Savage Art: A Biography of Jim Thompson*. New York: Alfred A. Knopf, 1995.

Polito, Robert, and Michael McCauley, eds. *Fireworks: The Lost Writings of Jim Thompson*. New York: Donald I. Fine, 1988.

Pronzini, Bill, ed. *The Arbor House Treasury of Detective and Mystery Stories from the Great Pulps*. New York: Arbor House, 1983.

Report of the Select Committee on Current Pornographic Materials. House Report No. 2510 pursuant to H.R. 596. 82nd Congress, 2nd Session. Washington, D.C.: U.S. Government Printing Office, 1952.

Ruehlmann, William. *Saint With a Gun: The Unlawful American Private Eye*. New York: New York University Press, 1974.

Ruhm, Herbert, ed. *The Hard-Boiled Detective: Stories from Black Mask Magazine, 1920-1951*. New York: Random House, 1977.

Sante, Luc. "Gentrification of Crime," *New York Review of Books*, March 28, 1985.

Schreuders, Piet. *Paperback, U.S.A.: A Graphic History, 1939-1959*. Translated by Josh Pachter. San Diego: Blue Dolphin, 1981.

Server, Lee. *Over My Dead Body: The Sensational Age of the American Paperback: 1945-1955*. San Francisco: Chronicle Books, 1994.

Shaw, Joseph T., ed. *The Hard-Boiled Omnibus: Early Stories from Black Mask*. New York: Simon & Schuster, 1946.

Shick, Frank. *The Paperbound Book in America*. New York: New York Public Library, 1958.

Silver, Alain and Elizabeth Ward. *Film Noir*. London: Secker & Warburg, 1979.

Tebbel, John. *A History of Book Publishing in the United States*, Vol. 3. New York: R. R. Bowker, 1978.

Tuska, Jon. *The Detective in Hollywood*. New York: Doubleday, 1978.

Utopia, No. 10: "American Paperback Cover Art." Rotterdam, The Netherlands: Utopia Foundation, 1978.

Index

The Story of Dutch Schultz
KILL THE DUTCHMAN!
Paul Sann
THE LUCIANO STORY
SID FED
JOACHI
JOESTE
THE STORY OF MY LIFE
CLARENCE DARROW
NEW INTRODUCTION BY ALAN M. DERSHOWITZ